6.50

GABLE

and

Lombard

WARREN G. HARRIS

SIMON AND SCHUSTER
NEW YORK

SBN 671-21744-5 Casebound
Library of Congress Catalog Card Number: 74-117
Manufactured in the United States of America

1 2 3 4 5 6 7 8 9 10

For Nana and our Saturdays at the movies;
for Mother, the first Gable fan I ever knew;
and for Lisa Ann, who likes a good story.

Contents

one

Going Home

Carole Lombard wanted to get home to Clark Gable as quickly as possible. They had been separated for a week, the longest they'd been apart since their marriage, nearly three years before. Though she was yearning to see him again, there was more to it than that. Knowing how susceptible he was to the advances of other women, she'd quarreled fiercely with Gable before she'd left about his relationship with Lana Turner, with whom he was starting a new picture.

It was January 15, 1942, a month after the United States entered the war. Carole Lombard was in Indianapolis, capital of her native state, winding up a cross-country tour to promote the sale of Government defense bonds. On that last day, she sat behind a desk in the rotunda of the State House for twelve hours, signing autographs and joking with the thousands of people lined up to meet her. Her quota had been set at $500,000, but she was such a persuasive saleswoman that she raised $2,107,513.

That night, Lombard attended a victory rally at Cadle Tabernacle, where, wearing a black strapless evening gown, with huge white roses embroidered on the scalloped skirt, she led the audience in singing "The Star Spangled Banner." Although the expensive dress, the bare shoulders, the long black gloves and the upswept blond hair were what the audience expected of a Hollywood star, that kind of glamour seemed eerily out of place in an auditorium decorated with patriotic banners urging everyone to "Sacrifice, Save and Serve!"

Carole Lombard started to cry when the national anthem was over. Thanking the crowd for making her tour so successful, she threw her arms in the air in a "V" formation. "Before I say goodbye to you all," she shouted, "come on and join me in a big cheer. V for Victory!"

Lombard, her mother, Bessie Peters, and an MGM press agent, Otto Winkler, had left Hollywood by train and were supposed to return the same way. But Lombard was in such a rush to get back to Gable that she told her companions she was too tired to face another three days of travel and tried to persuade them to take a plane instead.

Her mother had never flown before and was terrified by the prospect. Just before New Year's, the elderly woman's astrologer had advised her, "Stay off of planes in 1942." Otto Winkler, who was prone to airsickness, sided with Mrs. Peters and thought they could all use a few days of rest on the train.

Carole Lombard still held out for flying. She said the only fair way to settle it was to toss a coin. Winkler took an Indian-head nickel from his pocket and flipped it in the air. Heads, they would go by train, tails by plane. Lombard clapped her hands and squealed delightedly when the nickel landed tails up.

All planes were heavily booked because of the wartime emergency, but Winkler managed to get them on a TWA flight leaving Indianapolis at four in the morning and scheduled to arrive in Burbank, California, that same evening. It was the so-called "milk run," making numerous stops along the way, but it was the best Winkler could do. Ordinarily when accompanying someone of Carole Lombard's prominence, he had carte blanche in his choice of accommodations. As soon as he had made all the arrangements, he cabled MGM so that they would advise Clark Gable of the change in plans.

On the way to the airport, Lombard's mother suddenly realized that the date had advanced to January 16. A great believer in numerology as well as astrology, she knew that the number sixteen was a warning sign of an impending accident or death. She pleaded with her daughter to cancel their reservations. Lombard generally followed her mother's advice—she was as fascinated by the occult as was Mrs. Peters—but this time she was too fatigued and too impatient to get home to pay her much attention.

Her mother's anxiety increased when she studied the flight information and noticed the prevalence of the number three, which she also considered unlucky. The flight number was three and the aircraft was a Douglas DC-3. What made it even more ominous to Mrs. Peters was that they were a party of three people and that one of them—Carole—was thirty-three years old. Lombard, laughing at her mother's latest anxieties, told her that if she kept it up, there'd be a straitjacket waiting for her at the Burbank airport.

Once they were airborne, Mrs. Peters calmed down and tried to sleep, while Lombard passed the time studying the script of her next picture, "They All Kissed the Bride." Winkler had chosen a seat near the lavatory, in case he suddenly felt sick.

Boarding the plane in Wichita was concert violinist Joseph Szigeti, a Hungarian refugee who had just taken out his first U.S. citizenship papers and was headed for his new home in California. Szigeti didn't know who Lombard was, but he sensed she was someone important by the way other passengers were walking up and down the aisle trying to get a glimpse of her. He admired her black tailored suit and broadtail coat and was tempted to get the name of her dressmaker for his wife.

Szigeti was shy and unsure of his English. By the time he worked up enough courage to approach Lombard, the plane was getting ready to land at Albuquerque. During the stopover, Szigeti and three other passengers had to surrender their seats so that the plane could be filled to capacity with fifteen pilots and other men from the Army Ferrying Command, who had been ordered to return to their base in California as soon as possible.

TWA tried to get the Carole Lombard party to give up their seats to three more Army officers. Since this meant being stranded in Albuquerque overnight, Lombard pulled rank and insisted she had priority because she'd been on a Government mission. She disliked having to play the prima donna, but in this case she felt she was justified. She also didn't want to prolong her mother's anxiety over the flight any more than was necessary.

Flight Three generally flew nonstop between Albuquerque and Burbank, but this particular evening there was to be a landing at Las Vegas to refuel. Due to the increased passenger load at Albuquerque the plane was slightly overweight. This had been compensated for by reducing the fuel supply earlier.

Lombard was distressed by the sudden change in the flight schedule. Her mother's most anxious moments occurred during takeoff and landing. The stop at Las Vegas meant an extra round of moaning and hand-clutching for Mrs. Peters, whose nervousness was beginning to rub off on her daughter.

The plane landed at Las Vegas at 6:36 P.M., and after being serviced, took off again at 7:07. It was a clear, starry night as Carole Lombard looked out the window. Feeling the plane leveling off, she sighed with relief and patted her mother's hand reassuringly. They would soon be home.

"It'll sure be nice having Ma back. Life without her around ain't hardly worth living," Clark Gable said, watching the servants decorate the dining room with red, white and blue balloons and crepe-paper streamers. He had arranged a surprise dinner party for his wife and her companions, inviting his two brothers-in-law and Otto Winkler's wife to join them. There were bouquets of red roses in nearly every room. Gable wanted the house lighted only by candles when Carole Lombard arrived.

Upstairs in her bedroom, there was another surprise, to be shared only by the two of them. Lombard was a great practical joker. Just before she'd left on the bond tour, she'd placed the naked dummy of a blond woman in Gable's bed to keep him company. He got a big laugh out of it.

Now, to even the score, Gable had brought a male dummy home from the studio to put in his wife's bed. It was more realistic than hers, which had been a show-window mannequin. This naked male figure had a fully erect twelve-inch penis. Gable couldn't wait until Lombard pulled down the blanket on the bed and saw it. He knew exactly how she'd react, whooping and hollering obscenely and probably razzing him about how the dummy was better endowed than he was.

Gable looked at his watch. It was getting close to eight o'clock and he wondered why he hadn't heard from Larry Barbier, the MGM publicist who'd been sent to meet Carole Lombard's plane. Barbier was to have called him as soon as he knew the exact time of arrival. Gable wasn't going to the airport himself because of the photographers and reporters that would be there covering Lombard's return. He was proud of her for undertaking the bond tour and didn't want to steal any of the glory.

The phone rang. It was Eddie Mannix, second in command at MGM, and one of Gable's closest friends. "Can I call you back?" Gable asked. "I'm expecting word on Ma's arrival any minute."

"King, that's why I'm calling," Mannix said. "Larry Barbier just phoned from the airport. Carole's plane went down a few minutes after it left Las Vegas."

Gable blanched. "How bad do you think it is?"

"Nobody knows yet," Mannix said, "but we'd better get over to Vegas right away. The studio's chartering a plane. Someone will stop by in a few minutes to drive you to the airport."

All of the Gables' drinking glasses were king-sized. Gable filled one to the brim with Scotch and water and gulped it down to calm himself. The world always looked better to him through an alcoholic haze, but this time it wasn't going to help.

The night sky over the Nevada desert was still as clear as it had looked to Carole Lombard several hours earlier. From the porch of his bungalow at the El Rancho Vegas Hotel, Gable could see a reddish-orange light in the far distance, probably the burning wreckage of her plane.

A rescue party was already heading toward the glow, which was coming from the peak of 8,500-foot-high Mount Potosi, sometimes called Table Rock Mountain—but from this night on it would be known as Carole Lombard Mountain. There were no roads, only trails buried beneath hip-high snow, up to the summit. The seventy-year-old Indian guide leading the expedition said it might take twenty-four hours to reach the scene of the crash. Survivors, if there were any, would have to be carried down on stretchers or by mule train.

Gable arrived in Las Vegas too late to go with the first group of rescuers. He wanted to join the second group that was forming, but Eddie Mannix talked him out of it and went in his place. Mannix was terrified of what they would find up there and wanted to spare his friend. To persuade Gable to stay behind, he told him, "Suppose the first party brings Carole back and you're not here to greet her?"

"God damn it," Gable shouted. "I'll go mad if I can't do something about her." He spent the rest of the night locked in his bungalow, unable to go out because of the crowd of reporters and curiosity seekers who began hanging around the hotel as soon as word leaked out that Clark Gable was registered.

Although Howard Strickling, the head of MGM publicity, was there to keep him company, Gable said hardly a word the whole night. He was not an eloquent man to begin with, and his grief over his wife's almost certain death was more than he could cope with. Ignoring Strickling's suggestions that he try to get some sleep, he paced the floor, trembling and smoking one cigarette after another. Many hours later, a telegram came from Eddie Mannix, who'd sent it from a way station on the side of the mountain: "No survivors. All killed instantly."

Gable crushed the telegram in his hand and walked out on the porch. In the bright daylight, he could see the mountain clearly. He was not crying, but his sorrow was written all over his face. Deep circles ringed his eyes, and his color was as gray as the desert rocks. A sense of guilt over Carole Lombard's death was gradually overtaking him. He thought that if she hadn't been in such a hurry to get home to him, she would still be alive.

He went back inside and sat in a chair. His close friends, Al

Menasco and Buster Collier, who had driven out from their homes in California to be with him, tried to get him to eat but he refused. He even passed up their offer of Scotch or bourbon, saying he was numb enough without it.

"Why did Ma have to go?" Gable kept asking his friends. "Did you ever see anyone more beautiful? There was never a person in this world who was so generous, so full of fun. God damn it, why Ma?"

Carole Lombard's plane had collided headlong into a rock cliff, about 730 feet below the crest of the mountain, and had split in half upon impact. The front section, in which Lombard was seated, was compressed into a mass about ten feet long and partially consumed in the ensuing explosion.

When Eddie Mannix reached the wreckage, the air smelled of burning flesh and the snow was spattered with blood. There was almost nothing left of Carole Lombard. Charred remains thought to be hers would have to be identified by a comparison with X-rays of her teeth back in Los Angeles. All that Mannix could recognize were a few wisps of her light-blond hair, tangled in a piece of debris. A little later he found a pair of diamond-and-ruby ear clips, which he remembered Gable had given Lombard for Christmas. Missing and never found was a matching ruby pendant cut in the shape of a heart, also a gift from Gable. Legend developed that it had been embedded in Carole Lombard's own heart by the force of the crash.

When Mannix handed Lombard's clips to Gable as soon as he returned to the hotel, Gable faltered for a moment, but didn't break down, as Mannix thought he might. "Do you think she knew just before?" Gable asked.

"No," Mannix said. "It all happened too quickly." He told Gable that the trail to the scene of the accident was so narrow and treacherous that it would take two or three days to bring the bodies down. In the meantime, there was nothing more they could do but sit around and wait.

Gable asked to be driven out to the foot of the mountain.

When he got there, he walked off by himself to look for signs of the crash. They weren't hard to find. The burning plane had set off a forest fire in the ravine below it and the flames and smoke had left a black smudge all along the rocky cliffs surrounding the wreckage. Gable stood staring at it for several minutes. He had needed one final confirmation of Carole Lombard's death.

Back at the hotel bungalow, Gable retreated to his chair, where he sat for hours, completely oblivious of the friends who had gathered there. In the middle of the night, Buster Collier could stand the gloomy atmosphere no longer and insisted on taking Gable for a walk. They went out into the desert behind the hotel, where the cold, dry air invigorated Gable. When he went back inside, he asked for a drink for the first time since the long vigil had begun. The Scotch relaxed him. Halfway through his second glass, he started to reminisce about Carole Lombard and their life together. Those memories were to haunt him for the rest of his days.

two

A Case of Mutual Admiration

The Gable-Lombard romance ignited during a leap year, on Saturday night, January 25, 1936. The Mayfair Club of Hollywood was holding a formal ball called "The White Mayfair" at Victor Hugo's in Beverly Hills. All the women were requested to dress in white gowns, the men in white tie and tails.

Carole Lombard was overseeing the ball and serving as hostess. She'd wangled the job from producer David O. Selznick, president of the Mayfair Club, which was striving to bring a stately British tone to Hollywood's traditionally flamboyant night life.

Lombard was famous for throwing parties like the one in which she turned her house into a hospital ward and served dinner on an operating table. Although they were often derided as juvenile and undignified by such self-appointed social arbiters as Basil and Ouida Rathbone, they were always as funny and wacky as the hostess herself. She was too liberated and independent to really care what anyone thought. By taking on The White Mayfair, she hoped to prove that if she wanted to, Carole Lombard could toss a party just as grand and pretentious as those of Marion Davies, the Countess di Frasso and even the Rathbones themselves.

Lombard arrived early at the ball escorted by Cesar Romero, a last-minute replacement for her usual date, screenwriter Robert

Riskin, with whom she'd quarreled earlier in the week. She knew she'd be busy most of the evening, so she told Romero to circulate. One of the best dancers in Hollywood, he was tangoing to the strains of Eduardo Durante's Latin group with Virginia Bruce when Lombard next caught a glimpse of him.

Carole Lombard's table was near the entrance so that she could have a full view of the ball. Under her supervision, the inner and outer rooms had been lavishly decorated in white, with big bouquets of white roses, gardenias and sweet peas. It might have been a set for a Lombard movie, since white was the color generally used to highlight her pale hair and ivory complexion.

Six footmen in white jackets and red satin knee breeches were attending to the arriving guests. Three hundred and fifty people were expected, most of them stars and prominent industry figures, and they all seemed to be arriving at once: David Niven, Merle Oberon, Gloria Swanson, Janet Gaynor, Ernst Lubitsch, Harold Lloyd, Spencer Tracy, Louis B. Mayer, Dolores Del Rio, James Stewart, Bing Crosby, Darryl F. Zanuck, Jeanette MacDonald, Henry Fonda, Humphrey Bogart, Adolph Zukor, Claudette Colbert, Douglas Fairbanks, Barbara Stanwyck, Harry Cohn, Irene Dunne, Fredric March, Alice Faye, Jack L. Warner, Buster Keaton, Loretta Young. . . .

Like many others in the room, Lombard was surprised when she heard Young's name announced. Had the actress recovered from the illness that had forced her into temporary retirement right after making a picture with Clark Gable?

Gable himself walked in a few minutes later with Marion Davies' group. Davies was a discreet few steps ahead of her paramour, William Randolph Hearst, whose newspapers' gossip columnist, Louella Parsons, was tugging at his arm. Gable brought up the rear with his date, Eadie Adams, a blond singer who dubbed for Jean Harlow and other stars at MGM.

Lombard rushed over to greet Marion Davies, who was not only a close friend but also president of the Motion Picture Relief Fund, the beneficiary of the ball. She then shook hands with Hearst and kissed "Lollypops" (her pet name for Parsons). Gable flashed one of his honey-and-hemlock smiles at Lombard, and when he winked she winked back and gave him a reserved but friendly hello. It was the first time they'd met since making "No Man of Her Own" together four years before. That encounter had been a case of mutual dislike at first sight, he objecting to her boisterous behavior and profane vocabulary, she thinking he was too stuffy and reserved.

Now, from the way Gable was sizing Lombard up, he seemed to be having a change of heart. That tantalizing filmy white silk gown revealed the voluptuous contours of her body so clearly that she couldn't possibly be wearing anything underneath. Gable, impressed by how much more mature and self-assured she seemed, decided he would ask her to dance as soon as he'd fulfilled his obligations to Eadie Adams and Marion Davies.

If Lombard was having second thoughts about Gable, there was no time to analyze them. She suddenly saw red, literally as well as figuratively, as her eyes lit on Norma Shearer. Accustomed to having her own way as the queen bee of MGM, Shearer was flaunting a bright crimson gown. So far, only Jeanette MacDonald had ignored the request to come dressed in white. But MacDonald's mauve gown was too delicate a shade to clash with the surroundings. Shearer's did. Had it been one of Carole Lombard's own parties, she would have thrown Shearer out, but she didn't want to embarrass Shearer's husband, Irving Thalberg, one of the most respected men in the business.

As Lombard stormed into the powder room to calm down, she ran into Lupe Velez, the fiery Mexican wife of Johnny Weissmuller. Velez, who carried a stiletto in one of her garters, offered to "sleet" Shearer's throat when Lombard told her about the red dress. Lombard giggled and made a few obscene remarks about Shearer, recalling the gossip about her having been the mistress of Louis B. Mayer before she was passed down to Thalberg, his second in command. Velez, who had an even tougher vocabulary than Lombard, and used it with even less subtlety, tried to do her one better by adding more spice to the rumors, which had never been confirmed or denied by Shearer herself.

Lombard was still chuckling over her swearing match with Velez when she went back to her table to watch the dancing. She liked the way Cab Calloway, whose orchestra was alternating with Durante's group, bounced around the bandstand in his white swallowtail suit. The orchestra was playing the introduction to "Cheek to Cheek" when she noticed Clark Gable heading toward her, looking very dashing in his broad-shouldered tuxedo, but she detected an uneasiness and embarrassment about him as he spoke to her.

"I go for you, Ma," Gable said, grinning.

Lombard stared at him, puzzled, then suddenly realized that he was using one of the nicknames they'd given each other during "No Man of Her Own."

"I go for you, too, Pa," she said, though it didn't sound as if she meant it. Assuming he wanted to dance, she got up before he even asked her.

Gable was no Cesar Romero on the dance floor. He was holding Lombard so closely that he forgot about his feet, stepping on hers several times. He could tell now that she wasn't wearing any underwear. The closeness of their bodies and the scent of her Chanel Number 5 were arousing him.

Lombard couldn't help noticing. She threw her head back and laughed, opening her mouth wide. Gable's face reddened. She suggested they'd better sit down until he cooled off.

The dancing was ending anyway. Composer Irving Berlin sat down at the piano on the bandstand and played a medley of the new songs he'd written for Fred Astaire and Ginger Rogers' "Follow the Fleet." When the Latin band came on next, Lombard insisted that Gable do the rumba with her. The dance had become associated with Carole Lombard since she'd performed it with George Raft in a picture called "Rumba." Gable didn't know the steps, but she was a good teacher, and they won a small burst of applause from the crowd by the time they were finished.

Marion Davies, probably the busiest and most dedicated matchmaker in Hollywood, was watching Gable and Lombard's every move. Finally she turned to Louella Parsons and said, with her customary stammer, "Th-those two were m-made for each other. W-wouldn't it be g-great if they f-fell in love?" Parsons shrugged. She'd lost all faith in the permanence of movie-star romances since the divorce of Douglas Fairbanks and Mary Pickford, whose marriage she once described as "made in Heaven."

At a table across the room, another woman was seething at the sight of Gable and Lombard dancing together. She was Ria Langham Gable, his matronly second wife, from whom he was now legally separated. She still loved Gable and resented any threat to a possible reconciliation.

Ria glared icily at Gable and Lombard as they passed her on the way back to their own table. "Doesn't that old bag belong to you?" Lombard asked him when they sat down. Gable flushed again. He hated to be reminded of Mrs. Gable, who was trying to stall a final break by demanding a divorce settlement that would ruin him financially.

Gable said he needed some fresh air and offered to take Lombard for a drive in his Duesenberg convertible. At first she didn't want to go because of her obligations to the ball. But he looked so dejected that she finally gave in. After they had been driving for a few minutes, she noticed that they seemed to be circling around the Beverly Wilshire Hotel.

She asked Gable why, and he said he lived there. Would she like to come up to his apartment for a drink?

"Who do you think you are, Clark Gable?" Lombard quipped. That was all he needed—being reminded of the image the public had of him as the great lover who could have any woman he wanted. Disappointed and angered by her sarcasm, he slammed his foot on the accelerator and drove back to The White Mayfair at ninety miles an hour.

While Lombard rushed inside to check on the party, Gable stopped at the bar for a drink. Actor Lyle Talbot, who was standing at the bar, passed a snide remark that Gable didn't like. They were about to square off for a fight when Lombard came back and broke them up, dragging Gable off to dance.

Lombard was now in a fighting mood herself. Many of the

women were complaining about Norma Shearer's red dress and she wanted to tell the actress off. Gable talked her out of it, afraid that if the two women really got started on each other, the whole party would disintegrate into a free-for-all that would have to be described as "The Black and Blue Brawl" in the next morning's newspapers.

Cab Calloway's "Hi-De-Ho" swing band was playing a medley of songs made famous by Grace Moore. "One Night of Love" and "Love Me Forever" quickly restored Gable and Lombard to a romantic mood. He seemed to like holding her in his arms. Almost a foot shorter than he was, she looked comfortable leaning her head against his chest as she hummed along with the music.

Gable tried once more to persuade Lombard to leave the party with him, but she'd invited some of her friends to drop by her house for breakfast after the ball. She told him he was welcome, though, to come home with her to help prepare for her guests.

It was around twelve thirty when Gable and Lombard left for her house on Hollywood Boulevard. Since the ball wouldn't be over for several hours yet, he hoped he'd have some time alone with her.

Gable didn't stay very long. Lombard wanted him to serve as a combination butler and bartender, which was clearly not what he had in mind. She, of course, realized that, but wanted to make it plain to him that she was not to be had, at least for the time being.

When Gable used another appointment as an excuse to leave, Lombard asked him if it was with Loretta Young, which only made him angrier. He left in a huff, drove back to his hotel and went straight to bed after a couple of drinks.

The next morning, Gable was awakened by a strange cooing sound. Opening his eyes to find a plump white dove perched on his chest, he quickly closed them again, imagining he was hung over from the previous night's drinking. When he looked again, the dove was still there.

Gable sat up and looked around the room. On the table opposite him was a birdcage, the gate wide open. There was another dove roosting on the chandelier.

After he'd left Lombard's house, she decided she'd been too hard on him, so she called up a pet shop and had them send over a pair of doves as a peace offering. She then bribed one of the hotel clerks to release the doves in Gable's apartment while he was still asleep.

Gable was cursing as he tried to catch the doves and put them in their cage. He wondered who could have played such a dumb trick on him. Then he found a card attached to the leg of one of the birds, with the words "How about it? Carole." He laughed out loud, delighted to discover that he might have a chance with her after all.

Gable phoned Lombard. He apologized for being rude and thanked her for the doves, although he didn't know what he was supposed to do with them. His small apartment was beginning to smell like the birdhouse at the zoo.

Lombard offered to keep them at her house. She said he could come out to feed them every Sunday afternoon. Eager to see her again and perhaps pick up where they'd left off, Gable wanted to drive over with the doves immediately. But having no intention of making it that easy for him, she sent her butler to pick up the birds.

Gable kept calling Lombard for dates but she was always busy. They didn't see each other again until February 7, exactly two weeks after the Mayfair ball, at another party, this one concocted by Gable and a friend from MGM, screenwriter Donald Ogden Stewart. Over drinks one day, they decided they had to do something to cheer up Stewart's wife, who was recuperating from a nervous breakdown and forbidden to go out at night.

"Bea Stewart's Annual Nervous Breakdown Party" was called for high noon, at the home of millionaire John Hay Whitney. Even though it was called for midday, everyone was supposed to wear their gaudiest evening clothes to lend an extra air of lunacy to the gagged-up proceedings.

Shortly after noon, Gable was standing in the vestibule of the

Whitney mansion, welcoming the guests. As he was shaking hands with Robert Taylor, he heard the wailing sound of a siren. Rushing outside, Gable saw a white ambulance pulling up. Two uniformed attendants jumped out of the front seat and ran around to open the back doors. They climbed inside and emerged with a stretcher bearing a figure wrapped in a white sheet. Only her face was showing. It was Carole Lombard. Her eyes were closed and she seemed to be unconscious.

Stunned, Gable followed the attendants as they carried Lombard into the house and set her down in the middle of the living room. A crowd quickly gathered around the stretcher. Lombard looked so pale and helpless that Gable was afraid she'd been in a bad accident on the way to the party.

Suddenly Carole Lombard bolted upright and sat there laughing at everyone. Few people were amused, least of all Gable. Noticing the disapproval on their faces, Lombard shouted, "What the fuck's the matter with everybody? Can't you tell a gag when you see one?"

Gable glared at Lombard and walked away. He could hear her cursing. "I always knew Gable was a stuffed shit—I mean shirt," she said.

Gable turned and shouldered his way back through the crowd to Lombard, who had removed the sheet and was standing in a white evening gown. He grabbed her by the hand and led her to a quiet corner of the room.

He looked angry enough to slap Lombard as hard as he had Norma Shearer in "A Free Soul." Outraged at the way he had taken the edge off her gag, Lombard was herself ready to explode. It was no time for a heart-to-heart talk, but Gable tried anyway.

He told her that her joke was in the worst possible taste. She fired back that he had no sense of humor. He called her a screwy neurotic and she said he'd been turned into an old fogey by living too long with that "battle-ax" wife of his. Within a few minutes they were beginning to shout at each other. Lombard couldn't stand it any longer and walked away, leaving Gable sulking. As she passed Wallace Beery, she said, "That cocksucker's worse than a stuffed shirt. He's an insulting heel."

Lombard came out the winner of that encounter. As Gable reflected on what she said, he realized she was right. He definitely had lost his sense of humor. There had been little fun in his marriage to Ria Langham, a wealthy society woman. It had been a life of formality and pretentiousness, filled with stodgy socialites whose worst affectations he had unconsciously assumed.

Feeling that he owed Carole Lombard an apology, he looked around but couldn't find her. Kay Francis said she thought she'd seen her heading for the ladies' room. While he waited for her to return, Gable had a drink with Ronald Colman.

Gable lost all interest in Colman's description of his new yacht when he noticed Lombard coming back into the room, looking even more alluring than she had at The White Mayfair. Her white satin dress was less frilly and tighter fitting, and she had three white plumes stuck in her hair.

When she saw Gable, her blue eyes filled with hostility. He wanted to say he was sorry, but he was intimidated by all the noise and people around them. It would be useless to just ask her to go outside with him, so he suggested they play tennis. Dressed the way they were, in formal clothes, the idea was outrageous enough to appeal to her sense of humor and she accepted.

They spent most of the afternoon playing on the Whitney tennis court and they quickly worked off their mutual antagonisms in the excitement of the game. Gable, too big and clumsy to be a really good player, had to take off his jacket and unbutton his stiffly starched shirt to keep up with Lombard. She was laughing and joking wickedly through it all, never caring that her makeup was fading or that the plumes in her hair were drooping in the breeze.

When they finally stopped playing, Lombard had won every set, although she'd tried not to. She walked over to Gable's side of the net and saying, "I think I owe you something for that, Pa," she threw her arms around him, stood on her toes and kissed him. She then turned and ran back to the house, leaving a bewildered Gable to figure out where he went from there.

With Valentine's Day approaching, Lombard wanted to find an appropriate gift for Gable. She knew his fondness for fast cars and remembered that when he had taken her out in his $16,000 Duesenberg the night of the Mayfair ball, it had irked him that Gary Cooper owned the same model.

Deciding that as a Valentine's Day surprise she'd send Gable a car that would be uniquely his own, Carole Lombard went to a junkyard and for fifteen dollars bought a decrepit Model T Ford that was barely in running order. She then had it towed to a body shop, where it was painted white with big red hearts all over it.

On Valentine's morning, Lombard had the car delivered to Gable at MGM, where he was in the midst of rehearsals for "San Francisco." He knew it could only have come from Carole Lombard. A note on the steering wheel, "You're driving me crazy," confirmed it.

Thrilled with the car, Gable insisted on taking Spencer Tracy for a ride during the lunch break on the back lot, where "The Good Earth" was shooting. When the car sputtered and stopped, a group of Chinese peasant "extras" came along and pushed Gable and Tracy all the way back to their own set.

Gable considered sending Lombard a fire engine to reciprocate, but he dropped the idea when he learned how expensive it would be. Instead, he called her up and invited her to go dancing with him that night at the Trocadero.

Lombard spent the rest of the day getting ready. She decided to wear a beaded champagne-colored gown originally designed for one of her pictures. It was to be her first date with Gable and she wanted to dazzle all of Hollywood as they zoomed by in his open sports car.

But Gable had a surprise for Lombard. When he came to pick her up, instead of the Duesenberg, he was driving the Valentine jalopy. And despite its recently painted exterior, it was very shabby inside, with springs popping out of the seats.

Lombard was a good sport about it all. Wrapped in a white chinchilla jacket, she climbed into the old wreck as if it were a Rolls-Royce. Gable had done some quick repair work on the engine, but it still wasn't working well. They chugged down Hollywood Boulevard at ten miles an hour. They were both laughing heartily by the time they pulled up to the Trocadero.

The band was playing "You Were Meant for Me." As Gable took Lombard in his arms, she whispered, "Pa, they're playing our song." He listened for a moment and grinned. She was right.

three

Life Before Lombard

At that time, February 1936, Clark Gable had just
passed his thirty-fifth birthday. He was not yet called "The King of
Hollywood," but he certainly qualified for the title as the most
popular actor in the movies, the one against whom all others were
being measured.

To the public he was the Great American Dream Man of the
Depression era—rugged and virile, with an insolent grin and a
crackling staccato voice, who conquered both women and adversity
with a mixture of daring and brute force. But despite his public
image, created by his film roles and nurtured by publicity, the
real Gable was quite a different person.

He was born William Clark Gable, on February 1, 1901, in
the little mining town of Cadiz, Ohio. His father was an itinerant
oil driller, his mother a farmer's daughter and an epileptic who
died nine months after his birth. Gable was raised by an indulgent
stepmother who thoroughly spoiled him. He never seemed to out-
grow his dependency on her, and in later years he would always
need a strong woman around to run his life for him.

Only a fair student, Gable dropped out of high school in his
second year. His stepmother was seriously ill and his father returned from the oil fields to settle the family on a small farm.

William Gable hoped that the hard work and long hours would toughen his son and give him a sense of responsibility. But when he was sixteen, Clark was so unhappy that he ran away from home.

The next few years were the toughest of his life. Arriving in Akron, he got a job at the Firestone Tire and Rubber factory, molding treads on automobile tires. That turned out to be even more intolerable than the farm. Impressed by the apparently effortless and glamorous life of some actor friends, he decided to try out for a theatrical career. The only job he could find was as an unpaid "call boy"; his duties were to knock on dressing-room doors to tell the actors when to go on and to run errands between the acts.

When his stepmother died and Gable returned home for the funeral, his father forced him to go with him to Oklahoma, where there was an oil boom. There, Gable worked as a tool dresser until he reached twenty-one, when he told his father he was quitting to become an actor. The elder Gable considered acting an occupation fit only for sissies and they had a violent argument before Clark left. It was their last contact for many years.

Gable then joined a traveling repertory company as a roustabout. When the show was wiped out by a blizzard, he was stranded in Butte, Montana, with twenty-three cents in his pocket. He hoboed out of town on a freight train as far as Oregon, where he got a job at one end of a cross-cut saw in a lumber camp. On one of his few days off, he went to audition for a local theatrical group. Although he was too inept and inexperienced to qualify for even the smallest role, it was here that he met Frances Doerfler, a young actress who was to become the first woman since his stepmother to take him in hand. There were to be many more after her.

Sensing that Doerfler might be able to teach him some of the rudiments of acting, Gable made an awkward and obvious attempt at courting her. The actress caught on immediately. But as he persisted, she started feeling sorry for him and offered to coach him. The relationship quickly developed into Gable's first serious romance. He was an overeager, jealous lover, who threatened to kill himself whenever Doerfler even mentioned another man. It was hardly the type of role Clark Gable would have played on the screen.

With Doerfler's help, Gable started getting bit parts in local plays. Then, in 1923, he suddenly dumped her when he met a woman who was in a better position to help him. Josephine Dillon had been an actress on Broadway and now ran a drama school in Portland. She was thirty-six and unattached; Gable was twenty-two. He knew that if he didn't realize his acting ambitions soon, he'd have to spend the rest of his life doing some form of manual labor, since he had little schooling and no special skills.

It's doubtful that Gable succeeded in conning Josephine Dillon, a mature, college-educated woman, into a relationship she didn't want herself. For all his gaucherie and inexperience, he was tall and powerfully built, a lively, agreeable companion for a woman fourteen years his senior.

Dillon was the only dramatic teacher Gable ever had. He never paid for a single lesson—at least not in cash. Dillon worked on his crude diction, lowered his naturally high-pitched voice to a more resonant growl, showed him how to move more gracefully, taught him recitation and how to react to lines. She also improved his physical appearance, sending him to have his crooked, decaying teeth repaired and seeing to it that he gained weight. But there was nothing she could do for his floppy ears, which stood out from his head like jug handles.

Gable lived with Dillon for over a year, acting in some of the plays put on by her little theater group. In the summer of 1924, she moved to Los Angeles, hoping to find work as a coach in the theater or with some of the movie studios. Gable followed her there as soon as she was settled. A few days after his arrival, Dillon found him his first movie job, a three-day stint as an extra at Paramount in Ernst Lubitsch's "Forbidden Paradise." He received seven and a half dollars a day, playing a French grenadier in scenes with Pola Negri and Rod La Rocque. He realized more than ever now how much he needed Dillon, and on December 13, 1924, he married her.

The couple moved into a small twenty-dollar-a-month bungalow apartment, where Dillon supported them both by teaching drama students and reading scripts for some of the smaller movie studios. She bought Gable a secondhand car and sent him on the rounds of theatrical and movie casting offices. The results were discouraging. Romantic, handsome actors like John Gilbert, Rudolph Valentino and Douglas Fairbanks were then the rage. Hayseedy Gable, with his big hands and feet and rough-hewn face, couldn't even qualify for character parts. All he could manage was occasional work as an extra in such films as "The Merry Widow," "The Plastic Age" and "North Star."

Gable finally began to advance himself by becoming an outright stud to a couple of famous stage stars. Jane Cowl, thirty-nine and playing a fourteen-year-old heroine, issued a casting call for six-foot-tall spear carriers for her Los Angeles production of *Romeo and Juliet*. Admiring the way Gable carried his spear, Cowl hired him and invited him to dinner in her rooms after the show. He was soon promoted to the role of Mercutio.

Pauline Frederick, who was about the same age as Cowl, had a similar interest in advancing the careers of young men. When Gable was hired for the part of an old judge with a long white beard in her revival of *Madame X*, it wasn't a case of typecasting. Gable was also expected to play real love scenes with the actress in her apartment, while they were serenaded by gypsy musicians. After a week of such encounters, an exhausted Gable started complaining to some of the other actors, "Every night that woman acts like she never expected to see another man." When the affair ended with the closing of the play, Frederick expressed her appreciation by picking up the bill for some more of Gable's dental work.

When his wife learned of the affair, Gable very sheepishly moved into a furnished room by himself. Dillon took her husband's philandering philosophically. "He was never much interested in other women," she said later. "He did not go after them. They did all the pursuing, just could not leave him alone."

The most persistent of these women was forty-three-year-old Maria Franklin Prentiss Lucas Langham, a wealthy socialite. She was one of the backers of a Houston, Texas, stock company that hired Gable in 1927 and accounted for his taking temporary leave of Los Angeles. Ria Langham was a former Kentucky farm girl who had one child from an early teen-age marriage and two more from her subsequent union with a millionaire oilman. After the oilman's death, she married a prominent insurance broker, whom she divorced soon after meeting Gable.

Now twenty-six, Gable had filled out in face and form and exuded a raw sexuality that made him extremely popular with the Texas matrons who packed the theater whenever he appeared. Ria Langham wanted him the moment she saw him. When she arranged for him to be promoted from featured player to leading man and to have his salary raised from seventy-five to two hundred dollars a week, Gable reciprocated in the only way he knew how.

Their affair helped Gable a great deal, not only in furthering his career, but also in making a gentleman of him. Despite Josephine Dillon's influence, Gable was still a country bumpkin in many ways. Langham taught him table manners and social etiquette, developed his poise and showed him how to dress. For a time, until she toned him down, he was a real dandy, wearing a derby and spats and carrying a gold-knobbed cane.

In 1928, Langham rented an apartment on Fifth Avenue and took Gable to New York to help him get established on the Broadway stage. He landed one of the leading roles in *Machinal*, a drama that closed after twelve weeks. However, Gable's notices were strong enough for him to go on to *Gambling*, but author George M. Cohan fired him during the Philadelphia tryout and took over the role himself. Alice Brady, another of those maturing stars who preferred younger men, hired Gable for *Love, Honor and Betray*. The affair lasted no longer than the comedy's forty-five performances.

Josephine Dillon was appearing in a play in New York, but Gable refused to see her. She sent word to him asking if he wanted a divorce. He told a mutual friend, "What in hell do I want a divorce for? I never intend to get married again as long as I live. If she wants a divorce, let her get it!" So Dillon started divorce proceedings when she returned to California.

Gable went back to Los Angeles in June 1930, again with the

help of Ria Langham. She invested in the West Coast production of the Broadway stage hit *The Last Mile*, with the understanding that Gable would play the leading role of Killer Mears. The part of an embittered condemned man who leads a prison break had already made a star of Spencer Tracy. Ria hoped it would do the same for Gable. Seeming to throw all the resentment and frustration he had known in his own life into the character, his vivid, powerful performance created a sensation.

Lionel Barrymore, who had an actor-director contract at MGM, saw Gable's performance and arranged a screen test. However, Barrymore apparently had a very peculiar view of Gable's potential, covering his body with dark makeup, curling his hair and placing Gable before the camera wearing only a loincloth and a red hibiscus behind one ear. Irving Thalberg took one look at the scenes of Gable strutting around like a Polynesian prince and threw Barrymore out of the projection room, shouting "Good God, Lionel! No, not that! Take it away!"

But agents Ruth Collier and Minna Wallis offered to represent Gable on the basis of his work in *The Last Mile*. They arranged a successful screen test for him at Pathé, which cast him in the villain's role in a William Boyd Western, "The Painted Desert," at seven hundred and fifty dollars a week. Gable, eager to get the part, lied about his ability to ride a horse, and he had to hire an old cowboy to teach him before production started.

Director Mervyn LeRoy was preparing the movie version of the brutal gangster novel "Little Caesar" for Warner Brothers, and he made what he thought was an excellent screen test of Gable for the title role. When he showed it to the top executives, Jack L. Warner and Darryl F. Zanuck, they hated it. "Why do you throw away five hundred dollars of our money on a test of that big ape?" Warner ranted. "Didn't you see those ears when you talked to him? And those big feet and hands, not to mention that ugly face of his?" Edward G. Robinson finally got the part.

Feeling bad about the bungled screen test he'd made with Gable at MGM, Lionel Barrymore arranged a new one. This time Gable was carefully dressed in a well-tailored suit, and his ears were pulled closer to his head with fishskin. Just before the take, Barrymore whispered to Gable, "Keep your mouth closed, son, until you get those front teeth capped."

Irving Thalberg was more impressed by the new test. And since Barrymore seemed so sure he had a future, Gable was signed to a short-term MGM contract at three hundred and fifty dollars a week. His agents immediately sent him to a dentist to have his teeth capped, but the work was done quickly and carelessly, and he eventually had to have all his teeth, upper and lower, replaced with false ones—a fact that MGM always tried to keep secret for fear it would destroy his romantic image.

Gable's first film at MGM was "The Easiest Way"; he appeared in a minor role as Constance Bennett's brother-in-law, a laundryman. In "Dance, Fools, Dance," he played a bootlegger and killer opposite Joan Crawford. When they first met, "it was like an electric current went right through my whole body," Crawford said later. "There was a thing that went through the two of us like dynamite. . . . In the one scene where he grabbed me and threatened the life of my brother, his nearness had such impact, my knees buckled. If he hadn't held me by both shoulders, I'd have dropped."

That was the start of what one observer close to the scene described as "the affair that nearly burned Hollywood down." Crawford's marriage to Douglas Fairbanks, Jr., was being publicized as one of the most idyllic in Hollywood. But in the beginning, Crawford had been criticized for using it to further her career, becoming the daughter-in-law of the movies' "Royal Couple," Douglas Fairbanks and Mary Pickford.

Whether or not Gable saw Crawford as a means to boosting his own career, he fell in love with her. He was twenty-nine, she was twenty-six, one of the most idolized and desirable women in the world, and quite a change for him from the much older Josephine Dillon and Ria Langham. Gable was still involved with Langham and not yet divorced from Dillon. If that wasn't complication enough, Crawford had her own marriage to think about. Their romance was played out very discreetly.

Since MGM didn't have a clear idea of what it wanted to do

with Gable, he continued to play supporting roles as a villain until Crawford demanded him as her leading man. She'd just made "Complete Surrender" with John Mack Brown, but felt there was no chemistry between them, so she persuaded Louis B. Mayer to remake the picture as "Laughing Sinners," with Gable taking over Brown's role.

The Gable-Crawford affair was now being gossiped about all over Hollywood. Mayer didn't approve; Crawford was one of MGM's biggest box-office draws and any scandal might be ruinous. Since Gable was only a lowly contract player who had yet to prove his worth to the studio, Mayer warned him to stay out of Crawford's private life.

Mayer, probably the most powerful man in Hollywood, was not someone Gable could afford to oppose. Not knowing what to do next, finally, on March 29, 1931, he married Ria Langham. A few months later he discovered that, since Josephine Dillon's divorce decree had not become final until April 1, he had committed bigamy. A second ceremony was held on June 19 to make everything legal.

That same month, the release of "A Free Soul" boosted Gable's career. Norma Shearer, Leslie Howard and Lionel Barrymore were really the stars, but Gable stole the picture as Shearer's gangster lover. Gable's brutality towards Shearer, climaxed by a scene in which he slugged her in the face, jolted audiences. The fan mail, then considered an accurate barometer of public acceptance, was so heavy and favorable that Gable was assigned to a personality buildup.

MGM had been lacking a really top male star since the decline of Ramon Novarro and John Gilbert. But their dashing "Great Lover" images didn't suit Gable, so the studio started publicizing him as a rugged outdoorsy sportsman type. Gable had never hunted or fished before, but he learned how and found that he liked it. Gradually he developed such expertise that people assumed he'd been at it all his life.

Gable regretted now that he had married Ria. Middle-aged and the mother of three children from previous marriages, she was not the type of companion the public expected a romantic idol to have. Joan Crawford came nearer to that image. Their affair flamed up again when they made "Possessed" together. The situation was, in Crawford's words, "like living over a lighted powder keg." Gable wanted to divorce Ria Langham to marry her, but Crawford was afraid it wouldn't last, having seen too many marriages between stars fail because of the ego problems involved. This realization came too late to save her own marriage, and she and Douglas Fairbanks, Jr., were divorced the following year.

Gable made twelve pictures in 1931, an incredible record for one star even in those days of "factory" production. By the end of the year, he was being called "Valentino in Jack Dempsey's Body" and "The Great God Gable." He had started a new vogue for the he-man hero, whose fists and sarcastic wisecracks were his only weapons. He was one of the few stars to appeal both to men, who admired his mastery of the female, and to women, who, in those days, yearned to be mastered.

Yet, in his personal life, Gable was being thoroughly mastered by his wife. Mrs. Gable ran the house, picked his friends, even paid the bills for a time. By 1932, he was earning two thousand dollars a week. A naturally frugal man, due to the hard times he'd known most of his life, Gable was staggered by some of the expenses his wife was running up. She was reveling in his newfound fame, throwing lavish parties and insisting that he take her out to all the nightclubs and big premieres.

Gable's pictures were earning a fortune for MGM, yet Louis B. Mayer considered him a passing fad, "a gigolo with brass knuckles." When Gable started complaining about some of the roles he was playing, Mayer got so angry he disciplined him by lending him out to Columbia Pictures, considered a "Poverty Row" studio and the equivalent of Siberia for someone accustomed to the posh MGM setup. But Mayer's tactic backfired: the picture Gable made at Columbia was "It Happened One Night."

The Frank Capra "screwball" comedy was a sensational hit. It was one of the most influential films of the Thirties and eventually became a classic. For his portrayal of the brash, overly confident newspaper reporter, Gable won an Academy Award. The picture proved to Mayer and any other doubters that Gable had become a national phenomenon. Gable's apparent disdain for undershirts—he wore none when he undressed in one scene—caused retail sales of the item to plunge by 75 percent, and millions of men started sporting imitations of Gable's pencil-thin moustache. When Gable was sent on a cross-country personal-appearance tour, the crowds were the largest and most unruly since FDR announced he was shutting down the nation's banks for a day in 1933.

Gable's contract with MGM was due to expire. He had enough bargaining power to be able to sign a new seven-year contract starting at four thousand dollars a week, double his present salary. The raise sent his wife off on her wildest spending spree yet, and Gable was becoming increasingly unhappy in the relationship. Ria Gable had become so accustomed to running his life that she had taken to bossing him around in front of company, constantly criticizing his manners and clothes and reminding him to perform little chores the butler should have done.

Gable was away from home for nearly three months while filming "Call of the Wild" in an isolated snowbound area near Mount Baker, Washington. Rumors drifting back to Hollywood said he was having an affair with his leading lady, Loretta Young. When Young subsequently announced she was ill and retiring from the screen for a year, speculation was that she had become pregnant by Gable.

Gable's troubles with Ria deepened as his extramarital flings increased. The gossip columns and fan magazines were filled with his latest escapades with starlets, Broadway showgirls, even a debutante or two. Ria Gable said he was like a child who had suddenly been given too much candy. Often, after an argument with his wife, he'd pack a bag and move into a hotel room.

Gable fought against making "Mutiny on the Bounty," afraid that audiences would laugh at him as an Englishman in knee breeches and a pigtail, but MGM appeased him by sending him on a promotional tour of South America when it was over. Women made themselves so available during that trip that when Gable returned, he was in no mood to go back to his wife. After talking it over, they decided to separate. Gable moved permanently into the Beverly Wilshire Hotel. When the news broke, Gable would only tell reporters, "Mrs. Gable is a fine woman. Whatever fault there is, blame it on me." She attributed the break to Gable's always being under tremendous pressure. "It was a combination of too much work, too sudden success and the fact that women fairly threw themselves at him all the time," she said.

Gable had no intention of getting a divorce, at least for the time being. In the first place, he couldn't afford it. The community-property settlement that was part of the separation agreement was costing him two thousand dollars a week—half his salary. In the second, the separation was actually better than a divorce, not only enabling him to be seen openly with other women, but also giving him a convenient excuse for not marrying them if the romance became serious.

But he hadn't figured on falling in love with Carole Lombard.

four

The Madcap Miss Peters

When the romance started, Carole Lombard was twenty-seven. She had been under contract to Paramount Pictures for six years, working her way up from three hundred dollars a week to her present three thousand. Along with Mae West, Marlene Dietrich and Claudette Colbert, she was one of the studio's leading female stars.

She was born Jane Alice Peters on October 6, 1908, in Fort Wayne, Indiana, which was only about three hundred miles from Gable's home town. Although she came from a wealthy family, she never enjoyed many of the advantages of such a background. Her parents separated when she was seven, and her mother took the little girl and her two older brothers, Frederic and Stuart, to live in Los Angeles. While Mrs. Peters' allowance of four hundred dollars a month from her husband enabled her, in 1915, to provide quite adequately for the three children, it ruled out the private finishing-school type of education that Lombard would have had in Fort Wayne.

Lombard was a tomboy who trailed after her two brothers wherever they went, developing the same interests they had in baseball, football and other sports. She felt a great need to prove to them that she was their equal and never lost this competitive drive, which helped her to overcome many of the setbacks of later years. She was only an average student, but she had an impressive athletic record. She won medals in track and field, excelled at tennis, volley ball and swimming. Her physical training proved an asset in her movie career, developing her coordination and timing and also giving her a sense of fairness and respect toward others, which she always retained.

Carole Lombard made her first movie when she was twelve. The neighborhood boxing champ, she was sparring with her brothers in their back yard when director Allan Dwan visited some friends next door. Dwan was so captivated by the scrappy blonde that he obtained her mother's permission to cast her as Monte Blue's sister in "A Perfect Crime." The three-day job paid fifty dollars and it made her want to become a movie star like her favorites—Mary Pickford, Gloria Swanson, Colleen Moore and Norma and Constance Talmadge.

Lombard finished her formal education upon her graduation from junior high school. That put her about even with Gable in schooling, since he never finished the tenth grade. At fifteen, she enrolled in the Marian Nolks Dramatic School and joined a local amateur theatrical group called "The Potboilers." Through the influence of a family friend, she was screen-tested at Fox Films, which hired her to play Edmund Lowe's wife in "Marriage in Transit." Lombard was sixteen, her leading man thirty-three. To make her appear older her hair was darkened and she wore high-necked, long-sleeved dresses.

She was still known as Jane Peters, but Fox considered that too ordinary a name and asked her to change it. The Lombard was borrowed from neighbors of that name, and Carole was selected by her mother after consulting her numerologist. It started out as "Carol," the final "e" being added in 1930, when it was spelled that way by accident in the advertising for "Safety in Numbers." She kept the new spelling because she thought the extra letter would bring her luck.

Fox signed Lombard to a contract at seventy-five dollars a week. She was cowboy star Charles (Buck) Jones's leading lady in "Hearts and Spurs" and "Durand of the Badlands." Before Jones would agree to work with her, she had to pass a riding test. He put her on Re-Take, a horse that had appeared in so many pictures that it stopped short as soon as it was out of camera range. It took an experienced rider to avoid being pitched right over the horse's head when this happened—but Lombard managed it and won the part.

Lombard had already been taught a great many obscenities by her brothers, as protection against winding up on the so-called "Hollywood casting couch," and she expanded her vocabulary of profanities while working with Jones and his crew of hardened cowboys. Lombard once said, "If you're a young blonde around this man's town, you have to keep the wolf pack off somehow. If you know all those words, they figure you know your way around and they don't act quite so rough. It's better than having a black-snake whip in your hand."

Throughout all her life she used profanity freely, but never around children or her mother. She spoke that way for comic effect and to relieve tension on the set. Strangers were the only ones shocked by it, those who knew her accepting it as part of her personality. As one friend put it, "She could say, 'I don't give a shit' and it sounded as innocent as 'Isn't it a nice day?'"

Lombard didn't attract much notice opposite Buck Jones's Amazing Wonder Horse, Silver, and Fox soon dropped her. There were almost as many blonde starlets in Hollywood as there were oranges on the trees. Lombard would probably not have been able to withstand the competition, except for a seemingly tragic occurrence that changed the direction of her career.

As she and her boyfriend were returning home from a hockey game one night in 1926, his Bugatti sports car stopped short. Lombard was thrown against the windshield, which shattered and made a bone-deep cut extending from her left cheek to the corner of her mouth. The doctor who attended her warned her that using an anesthetic would relax her facial muscles, and that she might be disfigured for life. Since her career depended on her good looks, she submitted to the fourteen stitches without anything to relieve the pain. Her eyelids were then taped down and she was not permitted to move a muscle in her face for ten days. When the bandages were removed, there was an ugly crimson scar.

Lombard refused to see anyone but her family and close friends, remaining at home in seclusion for months. While she was recuperating she began to study lighting, photography and makeup so that she could minimize the effects of the scar. In time it gradually faded, and with subsequent plastic surgery it was hardly noticeable. But Lombard knew it was there, always reminding her of her narrow escape from disaster.

Hoping to snap her out of her depression from the accident, her mother sought the help of a friend who was a production manager at the Mack Sennett Studio. Lombard was hired as one of the Sennett "Bathing Beauties" at fifty dollars a week, since a good figure, rather than a pretty face, was the main qualification for the job. Thanks to her athletic training, Lombard had that, and in the few close-ups in Sennett's slapstick comedies the face was being hit with a custard pie or squirted by a seltzer bottle, so there was little chance of Lombard's scar's being noticed.

Although Sennett was long past his heyday in the early silent era, the thirteen two-reelers that Lombard made for him in 1927–28 helped to develop the comedy style and sense of timing that were so much a part of her later "screwball" phase. It was also at Sennett that Lombard met Madalynne Fields, a big, overstuffed dumpling who acted as a comic relief to the bathing beauties. "Fieldsie" had a sense of humor to match her size and was exactly the type of friend Lombard needed to cheer her up in those post-accident days.

When Sennett posted his closing notice, Fieldsie didn't see much future for herself. But she thought Lombard had promise, and she started acting as her unofficial manager. Rigged up in a slinky gown, false eyelashes and gobs of makeup, Lombard was hired to play a vamp in "The Divine Sinner." Though only a low-budget film made by a minor studio, it started Lombard's career rolling again. In 1928 she appeared in five pictures and was signed to a Pathé contract at one hundred and fifty dollars a week.

"High Voltage" was Lombard's first sound picture, and her distinctive silvery voice added an attractive dimension to her beauty. She was lucky in that respect, for many of the great silent stars, such as Pola Negri, Colleen Moore, Norma Talmadge, Mary Pickford and Clara Bow, were unable to make a successful transition to sound. New stars would be needed to take their places, and Lombard was determined to be one of them.

Although none of Lombard's Pathé pictures was very distinguished, working under directors like Raoul Walsh and Gregory La Cava gave her good experience. No one could get near Lombard now without first dealing with Fieldsie, her full-time secretary and business adviser. In June 1930, Fieldsie helped Lombard to negotiate a five-year contract with Paramount, roughly the same time that Gable was signing with MGM.

The move to Paramount was a propitious one, for it gave Lombard the backing of one of the biggest studios in Hollywood. Paramount had a full training program for its new contract players; Lombard was enrolled in dramatic, singing and dancing lessons. She needed this training if she was to compete successfully with such other newly signed Paramount actresses as Miriam Hopkins, Claudette Colbert and Sylvia Sidney, who had had extensive experience on the New York stage.

Lombard played chorus girls in her first two films at Paramount, and a secretary in her third. In "Man of the World," she graduated to a wealthy debutante, a role she might have played in real life if her parents hadn't broken up. During the filming, she fell in love with her leading man, William Powell.

Powell, at thirty-eight, was sixteen years older than Lombard. He was one of Hollywood's biggest stars and an experienced, polished actor. It's easy to see why Lombard, with her limited education and training, became enraptured of him. He was sophisticated and emotionally mature, witty and cultured in a way that Lombard aspired to be.

Paramount liked the Powell-Lombard team and rushed them into another picture together, "Ladies' Man." As their personal relationship developed, they had an odd effect on each other—she grew more serious and he became more playful. A lot of their time was spent socializing with Powell's best friends, actors Ronald Colman, Richard Barthelmess and Warner Baxter. They were known as The Three Musketeers and Powell was their D'Artagnan.

Powell wanted to marry Lombard, but she wasn't certain that the relationship could last because of the great difference in their ages. They lived together for eight months before deciding to legalize the union in a private ceremony in Lombard's home on June 26, 1931, just a week after Gable's marriage to Langham. The Powells sailed for Honolulu right after the ceremony, with Lombard promising friends she'd cable them the next morning with an account of the honeymoon night. Her message was crisp and to the point: "Nothing new to report."

Lombard's marriage to Powell strengthened her social standing in Hollywood. Their combined salary was over six thousand dollars a week. They lived on an extravagant scale that was beyond the imagination of the average American during those early Depression years. The marriage helped Lombard to acquire more poise, charm, and worldliness. But she was still childlike in many ways, unable to accept the responsibilities that went with being the mistress of a household. This presented problems right from the start. Powell also objected to her obscene vocabulary. When she wanted to annoy him in front of guests, every other word she uttered would be "shit."

Powell took himself very seriously, working hard at maintaining the cultivated, erudite image for which he was famous. It annoyed Lombard that he spent hours browsing through the dictionary to find big words he could impress people with. Apparently he played the celluloid William Powell twenty-four hours a day. Lombard told a friend, "The son of a bitch is acting even when he takes his pajamas off."

Lombard was too immersed in trying to save her failing marriage to take much notice of Clark Gable when they met for the first time in November 1932, for the making of "No Man of Her Own," which was to be their only picture together. Gable was on loan to Paramount from MGM, and he resented the preferential treatment Lombard got on her home lot. At the end of the filming, the gifts they exchanged seemed to express their negative feelings toward each other. Lombard gave Gable a big smoked ham with his picture printed on it. Gable reciprocated with a pair of over-sized ballet slippers, which he thought would fit a prima donna like his leading lady.

Lombard was making the aptly titled "Brief Moment" when she and Powell announced they were getting a divorce in August 1933. The marriage had lasted twenty-eight months. In the divorce action Lombard said that her husband was "a very emotional man, cruel and cross in manner of language, who displayed his temper repeatedly, almost from the day of marriage." Powell never told his side of it, but close friends said it was basically a matter of incompatibility: that Powell, at forty-one, wanted the kind of settled, ordered life that Lombard could not easily adapt to. But they remained good friends, largely because Lombard did not demand the huge divorce settlement customary in broken Holly-wood marriages.

Despite the failure in her personal life, Lombard was develop-ing into one of Paramount's important stars. Cast in a series of romantic melodramas, she was typed as an ultra-sophisticated but basically good-hearted glamour girl, who wore extravagant clothes and was always impeccably groomed. Components of the "Carole Lombard Look" were being widely copied by the young women who flocked to her pictures: high forehead, winging eyebrows, hollow cheeks, billowy hair. Few women, though, could match her curvaceous figure, which was usually encased in skintight evening gowns that revealed as much as the censors would permit.

Lombard was also extremely popular with her co-workers. Adolph Zukor, the head of Paramount, said that if he had taken a vote for Queen of the Lot, Lombard would have won by a land-slide. A fun-loving and completely natural woman, devoid of any of the bitchiness that was so characteristic of many of her con-temporaries, she was interested in everybody, regardless of how important they were, and she spread a spirit of good feeling that had actors and technicians vying to be assigned to her pictures.

After her divorce, Lombard became involved with Russ Columbo, the twenty-five-year-old singer noted for his intimate, throaty voice and the sexy way he rolled his eyes while singing "Prisoner of Love" and other sentimental ballads. Lombard used to tease him about his striking resemblance to Rudolph Valentino. He spent two hundred dollars a week on hair and sun-lamp treatments to retain his swarthy "Latin Lover" appearance. Like Valentino, he carried a mirror in his pocket and had no inhibitions about gazing at himself in public. This led, as it also did in Valentino's case, to considerable speculation about his masculinity.

Though what brought Lombard and Columbo together was a mystery even to some of their friends, each fulfilled a need in the other's life at that time. Lombard required an escort to squire her around to all those parties and nightclubs she enjoyed so much. She also liked to help people when they were down on their luck—as she herself had been after her accident—which might be another reason why she was drawn to Columbo. For several years, he had not been able to achieve any success in movies, as Bing Crosby and Rudy Vallee had done.

Lombard and Columbo saw a great deal of each other for over a year. Columbo even coached her for the two songs she had in "White Woman," in which she played a nightclub entertainer stranded on a rubber plantation in Malaya. Lombard would often invite Columbo to the set to watch production and pick up pointers that might help his movie career. But he stayed away from the filming of "We're Not Dressing" for fear of running into his rival, Lombard's leading man, Bing Crosby.

After that film, Paramount sent Lombard to Columbia Pictures for what was to be another turning point in her career. It was the film version of Ben Hecht and Charles MacArthur's Broadway comedy, *Twentieth Century*, which was to do as much for Lombard's popularity as "It Happened One Night" did for Gable's. Ironically, both films were made on loan-outs to the same studio and only months apart.

Lombard's leading man was John Barrymore, whom many considered America's finest actor, even though his best days were behind him because of his heavy drinking. On the first day of shooting, Lombard's performance was so stiff and disappointing that Barrymore tried to get her fired. Director Howard Hawks took time out to teach Lombard the importance of being natural and of improvising her own reactions to whatever happened to her in the script. She improved so much that Barrymore called her "the finest actress I have worked with, bar none."

When "Twentieth Century" was released in May 1934, Lombard received the best reviews of her career for her portrayal of the lingerie salesgirl who is transformed into a famous stage and movie star. With its emphasis on wackiness and sophisticated slapstick, the film was one of the first and best of the "screwball" comedies. As the genre became more popular, Lombard was to become its foremost practitioner. But in the meantime, fresh from her triumph with John Barrymore, she had to suffer the indignity of returning to Paramount for "Now and Forever," in which every scene was to be stolen from her by a six-year-old named Shirley Temple.

Lombard was vacationing at Lake Arrowhead on the Labor Day weekend of 1934 when one of Hollywood's most bizarre tragedies, the death of Russ Columbo, occurred. Columbo had been visiting his best friend, Lansing Brown, Jr., a young portrait photographer who had a collection of antique guns. He said he was absentmindedly playing with one when it fired and "Russ went down with a scream." The police investigation showed that the bullet ricocheted off the floor and a marble tabletop and then struck Columbo in the forehead, killing him instantly. A servant reported that he'd heard Columbo and Brown arguing violently just before the gunshot, but the case was finally written off as an accidental death.

Lombard rushed back from Lake Arrowhead for the funeral, at which her brother Stuart was one of the pallbearers. A blanket of gardenias from Lombard decorated Columbo's coffin. Outside the church, she told reporters, "His love for me was the kind that rarely comes to any woman." When Lombard found out that Lansing Brown was afraid to see her, she sent for him and said,

"Don't be silly. I know you loved Russ. I don't blame you. It was an accident. Russ would want us to go on being friendly, and of course we will."

Lombard had never seriously considered marrying Columbo. Her friends dismissed the affair as silly and without stature, but she wore mourning for him and seemed emotionally affected by the tragedy. Like the automobile accident, it was another reminder of her own mortality.

At the same time she was becoming unhappy with the progress of her career. After her success in "Twentieth Century," she saw her future as a comedienne. But when Paramount didn't agree and continued to cast her in one nondescript drama after another, she started complaining and refusing roles. Some she had to play, if she didn't want to go on suspension without pay. After "Rumba," in which she was a society girl mixed up with gigolo George Raft, she was sidelined for nine months, while Paramount underwent an internal reorganization.

During this period, Lombard reassessed herself and decided that the reason she was having so much trouble getting the kind of comedy roles she wanted was that Hollywood took her too seriously. They still thought of her as the dignified Mrs. William Powell, forgetting she was once a Mack Sennett girl. When a friend told her, "Drop that stuffed-shirt business and cut loose like you do in your own parlor," she followed the advice.

Lombard made herself into one of the most madcap characters Hollywood had ever known. If she was going to play screwballs on the screen, she might as well become one in real life. It wasn't a difficult part to play, simply an exaggerated extension of her own innate sense of fun and absurdity. As a writer of that period put it, "Carole went crazier and crazier. She was coarse, cynical, screaming, daft, all for the sake of craziness. For the sake of publicity, she was forever inventing newer and more spectacular public stupidities." It wasn't long before she was being rated "America's Madcap Playgirl Number 1." Lombard's nutty parties became one of her trademarks. The first was held in honor of William Haines, the former MGM star who had become an interior decorator. After he'd redone her house on Hollywood Boulevard, Lombard told Haines she would throw a party to show everyone what good work he did. Before the guests arrived, Lombard stripped the house bare. She laughed at everyone's startled reactions to Haines's apparent lack of talent and then invited them all back several nights later to the real party.

Robert Riskin, the writer of "It Happened One Night" and many other popular films, dated Lombard frequently, though they were never a serious romance. She thought he was a genius but that he worked too hard. On his birthday she staged a hayloft party in her living room. The floor was covered knee-deep in hay, with a couple of mules and a hillbilly band thrown in for atmosphere.

For her most famous party, Lombard hired the fun house at the Venice Amusement Pier and invited everyone she could think of, from stars and studio heads to messenger boys and cleaning women, urging them all to come in old clothes so there'd be no class distinctions. Some of Hollywood's snobbier personalities declined her invitation when they discovered they'd be mingling with grips, cameramen and others lower down the studio social scale.

Lombard's new carefree image started to bring results. When Ernst Lubitsch took charge of Paramount production in 1935, he cast her in "Hands Across the Table," a lighthearted comedy in which she had the unglamorous role of a fortune-hunting manicurist. Lombard's performance displayed a breezy tartness that was very appealing. Critics noticed that she had shed much of the false glamour and sophistication that burdened many of her earlier films.

"Hands Across the Table" was Lombard's most successful picture for Paramount. She went straight on to another comedy, "Love Before Breakfast," which she had just completed when her romance with Clark Gable started. After that, her career was never again to be the most important thing in her life.

five

A Three-Year Love Affair

"All her life, Carole Lombard had been running a race with a swift, invisible opponent. I think she always knew that she would never live to be old," a friend once said. "In all the time I knew her, I never heard her make any plans for her own future. She did not expect to follow the long trail. Perhaps that is why she tried to cram so much into her life, why she seemed to savor life—and particularly her life after she met Clark Gable—as few people ever did."

In the early part of 1936, Hollywood did not take the Gable-Lombard romance very seriously. Clark Gable had been involved with too many women for anyone to believe that he could settle down with only one, least of all the reckless and impulsive Carole Lombard.

But as it turned out, Gable and Lombard became lovers for more than three years. Their affair actually lasted longer than their marriage, though, of course, they didn't plan it that way. The situation was largely Gable's doing. In the midst of an unpleasant property squabble with his second wife, he was neither willing nor able to enter into another marriage.

The affair developed slowly, with Lombard deliberately taking her time with Gable. All too aware of his reputation for using women, she wanted to be certain that he was genuinely in love with her, that he had no ulterior motives.

Before she became too deeply involved with Gable, Lombard also needed to sort out her own feelings toward him. Whether she realized it or not, one of his main attractions for her was the fact that he was Clark Gable. Lombard always had to be the best in everything, whether it was as the child boxing champion of her neighborhood or as a major Hollywood celebrity. By capturing the man who was the most idolized movie star in the world at that time, she once again would be proving herself a winner.

But it would be a shallow victory if Gable did not have qualities that were compatible with hers. Her unsatisfactory marriage to William Powell had taught her that falling in love with a man's public image wasn't basis enough for a lasting relationship.

Lombard admired Gable's honesty and his ability to see people for what they were. While she felt hurt at the time it happened, she admired Gable for the way he told her off about her ambulance-and-stretcher arrival at "Bea Stewart's Annual Nervous Breakdown Party." Shortly after that confrontation, Lombard told an acquaintance that Gable "had my number so fast, it was terrifying. He told me what I was—a screwy, neurotic, miserable fool—and he was right. I've never been anything else. I've never had dignity or inside poise, or whatever it takes. I just fooled people. But I couldn't fool him, and I knew it. And so I hated him. And—oh, well—loved him, too."

As Lombard grew closer to Gable, she found him to be gentle, unassuming and a little shy, nowhere near as dashing or extroverted as his screen image. He was a rather lonely and sad man, who had never enjoyed real companionship during his two marriages to much older women and had never known the satisfaction of a lasting romantic relationship with a woman who was his peer. But his involvement with Lombard was to change all that.

At first the Gable-Lombard relationship seemed to please nobody except the two most concerned. MGM was furious, believing it would hurt Gable's popularity, particularly among women movie-goers. Though separated from Ria Gable, he was still legally her husband, and Louis B. Mayer, a great believer in the sanctity of home and family, didn't approve of a married man's being seen with other women. Mayer was old-fashioned enough to think that the public would turn against Gable if his affair with Lombard became too blatant.

Lombard had to face the same kind of opposition from Paramount, even though that studio was not nearly as protective of its stars as was MGM. She had a more difficult time with some of her friends, who advised her against getting too serious with Gable, warning her that it might not work out, that he might never be free of Ria Gable.

At that point, the Gable-Lombard situation appeared to one observer "like a kind of Romeo and Juliet in very modern dress. Maybe we all felt that way because the marks of greatness and tragedy and recklessness were on that romance from its start. And maybe, even while we disapproved so violently, we also realized instinctively that nobody had ever approved much of Romeo and his girl friend either. Not while they were alive."

For a time, the development of the affair was retarded by their preoccupation with their careers, Lombard committed to making "The Princess Comes Across" and "My Man Godfrey," while Gable had a similar lineup with "San Francisco" and "Cain and Mabel." Lombard was frail and tired easily. Rising at dawn each morning to get to the studio for makeup and wardrobe, she insisted on being in bed by eight thirty at night to conserve her energy. This severely restricted her social engagements.

Once and sometimes twice a week, she managed to see Gable for an early dinner at her house or at the Brown Derby. Lombard liked to catch up on all the studio gossip. While Gable was really not one to carry tales, he shared with Lombard a great relish in sending up the temper tantrums and power plays of some of their fellow stars.

Gable was amused by Lombard's accounts of her feud with George Raft over "The Princess Comes Across." Claiming that the cameraman was giving Lombard preferential treatment, Raft wanted him replaced. Lombard, who'd been working with the disputed cameraman, Ted Tetzlaff, for two years, was not about to give up an artist who knew exactly how to light her face and conceal her scar. Paramount sided with Lombard, instead replacing Raft with Fred MacMurray.

Gable told Lombard of his own problems with Jeanette Mac-Donald, who was known around MGM as "The Iron Butterfly." MacDonald had used her influence with Louis B. Mayer to force Gable into making "San Francisco" against his will. Lombard advised Gable that the only way to handle such a prima donna was to look right through her and pretend she wasn't there. The suggestion worked; Gable had no more trouble with his leading lady after that.

Gable would often rave to Lombard about his new friend, Spencer Tracy. Though they'd seen each other around MGM, they had never worked together until the filming of "San Francisco." The two actors, who both owed their start in movies to their stage portrayals of Killer Mears in *The Last Mile*, discovered they had something else in common, though it was not the sort of thing Gable would have discussed with Lombard. Both Gable and Tracy had, at different times, been involved with Loretta Young.

Gable found a real drinking buddy in Tracy. While alcoholic consumption was officially frowned upon by the studio during working hours, Gable and Tracy regularly dropped into each other's dressing rooms for a shot or two. Gable could drink all day and not show it, but Tracy would usually turn ugly and argumentative. Gable would put the bottle away then, as he wanted to avoid any trouble with Louis B. Mayer, whose secretary, Ida Koverman, was always snooping around the sets looking for infractions of the rules.

When Lombard was working, Saturday night was the only time that she would stay out late with Gable. He often took her dancing at the Trocadero or the Ambassador Hotel's Cocoanut Grove. Lombard had a sentimental attachment for the Grove. As a teen-age "flapper," competing in the weekly dance contests that were a tradition there, she won so often that she had a deal with the management to sell them back the trophy each time for fifteen dollars.

That was all behind her now. When she and Gable swept into the Grove, they were treated like royalty. Press photographers' flashbulbs would pop and the orchestra would dedicate "I Only Have Eyes For You" or some other current hit song to them. Lombard basked in the attention, but Gable's ears would turn red from embarrassment.

Gable and Lombard liked to spend their Sundays together away from the Hollywood crowd, usually driving to a dude ranch, where they hired horses and spent most of the day riding. They often attended rodeos and horse shows, but eventually had to give them up when they discovered they were attracting larger audiences than the featured events.

Even if they hadn't been Clark Gable and Carole Lombard, they would have stood out in any crowd. She was considered one of the best-dressed women in Hollywood—some said *the* best since the death of Lilyan Tashman in 1934. Most of the clothes in Lombard's personal wardrobe were designed by Travis Banton, one of her closest friends and Paramount's head fashion stylist. She was always impeccably groomed; she wouldn't even leave the house for a quick errand without making sure that her outfit and makeup were exactly right. Gable had that same kind of fastidiousness about himself, probably a reaction against his seedy, deprived early years. Like Lombard, he was a fashion plate. Noted for his natty sports clothes, he had started national fads for turtleneck shirts and unusual hats.

After their all-too-brief weekend, it was back to the hectic studio routine. Even though "The Princess Comes Across" still had two weeks of shooting, Lombard had finished all of her scenes and started on "My Man Godfrey." Made on loan-out to Universal, the film was filled with reminders of both Lombard and Gable's pasts. Playing opposite Lombard was her former husband, William Powell, with whom she had remained good friends, and who, in fact, was responsible for Lombard's being signed for "My Man

Godfrey," insisting that she was the only actress in Hollywood who could do full justice to portraying the screwball heroine.

William Powell was now in the midst of a two-year love affair with Jean Harlow, who was often teamed with Gable at MGM. Gable and Harlow were also very close friends. Lombard suspected they had once been lovers, but Gable would never admit to it.

Lombard was amused that fluttery Alice Brady, who it was known had once been involved with Gable, was playing her mother in "My Man Godfrey." When Lombard asked Brady for pointers on how to handle Gable, Brady couldn't remember many details of that brief affair seven years before when she had worked with Gable on Broadway. Brady had been involved with too many other men since, and apparently there was nothing special about Gable to make him stand out in her memory.

While "My Man Godfrey" was being filmed, Gable finished "San Francisco" and moved on to "Cain and Mabel." His co-star, Marion Davies, generally expected her leading men to attend to her personal whims as well. But she made no demands on Gable, out of respect for Carole Lombard, an old friend. Davies had sported with Gable before, anyway, when they had made "Polly of the Circus" in 1932. The only demand that she made of Gable now was that he shave off his moustache. It tickled her in their love scenes and made her laugh.

William Randolph Hearst, Marion Davies' lover and sponsor, was always attempting to prove to the world that she was more than just a superb comedienne. In "Cain and Mabel," Hearst was trying to turn her into a musical-comedy star. The production numbers were so elaborate that the roof of the block-long sound stage had to be raised 30 feet, at a cost of $100,000. In one scene in which Marion Davies wore a Venetian wedding dress made of 185 yards of satin and lace, she stood against a backdrop of a 90-foot-high church organ with 160 pipes, each adorned with a chorus girl dressed as a bridesmaid.

Gable considered himself lucky that in those scenes all he had to do was to be photographed sitting in a theater box seat looking adoringly at Marion Davies. He knew Lombard wouldn't believe the extravagant lunacy of it all unless she saw it for herself, so he invited her to visit the studio right after she finished "My Man Godfrey."

Marion Davies had her own little four-piece orchestra on the set to strike a happy mood during the long breaks between camera setups. When Gable and Lombard walked on, Davies told the musicians to play "Let's Make Hay While the Sun Shines."

At the end of the day, Gable and Lombard took Davies out to the Venice Amusement Pier to ride the roller coaster. The lovers held hands and necked in the front seat, while Davies sat alone behind them, laughing and screaming until she was hoarse.

Gable went off in a hunting trip when "Cain and Mabel" was completed. Since Lombard was also free, he tried to persuade her to go with him. But as much as she liked Gable, she didn't yet trust herself alone with him for an extended period of time, and she refused. Not wanting to discourage him too much, she told him to bring her back something cuddly, like a kitten. She loved animals and had a houseful of dogs, cats, chickens, ducks, goldfish and, of course, the doves she was keeping for Gable.

With a Mormon guide who'd once worked for Teddy Roosevelt, Gable spent ten days camping around the area of the Kaibab Plateau, on the northern rim of the Grand Canyon. He enjoyed the outdoor life—hiking, living in tents, cooking over an open fire—more than the actual hunting. He was an excellent shot, but felt that gave him an unfair advantage over his prey, and he would never fire at an animal while it was standing still.

Gable's guide tried to teach him the art of treeing cougars, which involved chasing one of those ferocious mountain lions up a tree and taking it alive by lassoing it around its neck and tail end. This proved to be beyond Gable's abilities, especially the lassoing, which took years to master. He did manage to capture a cougar, though, quite by accident. A cub came wandering into camp one night in search of its mother, which the guide had treed the night before.

Even though it weighed seventy-five pounds, Gable decided

that the cougar cub definitely qualified as a kitten. He brought it home to Carole Lombard. She was delighted with it, at least for the first few days. But the cub created such havoc in her little menagerie of domesticated pets that Gable finally donated it to the MGM zoo.

Gable had some other odd ways of expressing his affection for Lombard. Soon after the cub, he gave her a shrunken head, which natives had presented to him on a sightseeing trip up the Amazon during his South American tour two years before. Lombard said the head reminded her too much of George Raft, and she stuck it in a drawer where she wouldn't have to look at it.

Gable and Lombard were dating more frequently, now that she wasn't working. There wasn't a movie premiere or nightclub opening they missed. They both liked sports, and were seen frequently at the racetrack, the tennis matches and the major boxing and wrestling events. The gossip columnists started taking the couple a little more seriously. One said, "Probably the thing which makes them enjoy one another is the fact that they're both a little drunk on freedom and are dramatizing their freedom phases together."

But Lombard was becoming increasingly marriage-minded. Whenever she brought up the subject, Gable dismissed it, claiming that he couldn't afford his wife's demands for a divorce. But Lombard started to doubt his sincerity. Rumors were circulating that Ria Gable was bragging that her husband had begged her not to divorce him, that he was having too much fun in his semi-married state.

Although Lombard didn't take the gossip too seriously, she fumed when she read a magazine interview in which Gable said he'd probably never get married again. He claimed that no wife could ever put up with all the women who were constantly chasing him. Since Lombard concluded that Gable included her as one of those women, she didn't want anyone to get the impression that she was chasing Gable. So the next time he turned up at her house, she told him off and then threw him out.

Gable, dumbfounded, sat out front in his open car until three in the morning. Lombard finally felt sorry for him out there in the cold and invited him back inside for coffee. When she explained the reason for her anger in more detail, Gable apologized and said he couldn't blame her. He excused the magazine article as a plant by the MGM publicity department and promised to do his best to settle his problems with Ria Gable.

Lombard got flighty ideas at times. While she and Gable were making up that night, she suddenly thought that the shrunken head he'd given her was putting a hex on them and she insisted that they get rid of it immediately. Gable took her out for a drive and she threw the head in a vacant lot. Halfway home, she thought there might be trouble if it was found and traced back to them. They spent the next couple of hours thrashing through weeds and bushes until they retrieved the curio. Later, passing an empty house, Lombard made Gable stop the car while she ran out and buried the head in the back yard.

Lombard might have had a point about the shrunken head's evil influence, for after its burial her luck seemed to change almost immediately. When "My Man Godfrey" was released, it proved one of the high points of her entire career. Portraying a zany millionaire's daughter who picks up one of the Depression era's forgotten men in a charity scavenger hunt, she falls in love with him when she hires him as the family butler. Lombard's reviews surpassed even those she'd received for "Twentieth Century." The farce, a box-office smash, helped make Lombard the most sought-after comedienne in Hollywood.

"My Man Godfrey" also greatly impressed Gable when he saw it. He always told friends that Lombard's delightful performance was what finally made him realize that he had fallen in love with her.

The film's success came at a fortunate time for Lombard, who was negotiating a new contract with Paramount. Suddenly become what the industry trade papers liked to call "a hot box-office attraction," she could now get almost anything she demanded. Earlier in the year, Paramount had considered dropping her because her pictures weren't doing enough business to warrant her

$3,000 a week salary. She now tried to make it as hard on the studio as she could, to get even for its lack of confidence in her.

Lombard's new Paramount contract called for $150,000 per picture, making her the highest-paid female star in Hollywood. She also received concessions never before granted, earning for herself a reputation as one of the shrewdest businesswomen in the industry. She obtained the right to choose her cameraman and to be consulted on the selection of the director and supporting cast. She was allowed to make one independent picture a year. She was permitted to drive her car right onto the lot, instead of leaving it in the studio parking space. Moreover, she could select her own hairdresser and makeup artist, as well as any additional technicians she thought she needed. One of the latter was an electrician, Pat Drew, who'd lost a leg in a plane crash while working for Paramount on "Annapolis Farewell." Drew couldn't move well on his new artificial leg, and Paramount was trying to fire him when Lombard found out about it and insisted that Drew be assigned to all of her pictures. To thank her for such a gesture was impossible. "Get away from me," she'd say. She did things for people unselfishly, without wanting to talk about it.

Before Lombard would sign her new contract, she insisted that Paramount strike out the clause that gave them the right to dismiss her on grounds of "moral turpitude." She told the head studio executives that they had no right to interfere in her life as long as she did the job she was being paid for. Secretly she was afraid that if her affair with Gable ever developed into a public scandal, Paramount would have grounds for dismissing her on the spot.

The studio didn't want to delete the morals clause, which had been standard procedure since Clara Bow's celebrated orgy with the entire USC football squad. But Lombard was so adamant about removing the clause that Paramount finally acceded to her demands.

Lombard's new contract made Gable envious. He was MGM's exclusive property—he could work at no other studio and had little voice in the films he made or the people he worked with. He was unhappy over the direction his career was taking. "San Francisco" was very successful, but after the fiasco of "Cain and Mabel," he was saddled with "Love on the Run," a poor imitation of "It Happened One Night." The new film reunited Gable with Joan Crawford. Lombard worried about a flare-up of the old Gable-Crawford romance, but this time the former lovers had a chaperone in Crawford's new husband, Franchot Tone, who was also appearing in the picture.

Gable was making "Love on the Run" when Irving Thalberg died of lobar pneumonia, aged thirty-seven. Louis B. Mayer declared an official day of mourning for his former production chief. All studio activities at MGM were suspended for twenty-four hours.

Gable was selected to serve as an usher at the funeral services, even though he and Thalberg had never been very close. Gable blamed his lack of progress in his early years at MGM on Thalberg, who was more interested in promoting the careers of the female stars, particularly Greta Garbo, Joan Crawford, Jean Harlow, and his wife, Norma Shearer. Gable's career at MGM really didn't start building until after Thalberg became seriously ill in 1933 and stepped down into a less taxing job as head of his own production unit. When Thalberg finally realized the important star Gable was and used him in his own, personally supervised production of "Mutiny on the Bounty," it was too late for Gable to change his ambivalent attitude toward him.

Thalberg's death left Louis B. Mayer the absolute, unchallenged monarch of MGM. It also signaled the start of more than two years of conflict and intrigue between Mayer and his son-in-law, David O. Selznick, over "Gone With the Wind," with Clark Gable caught right in the middle.

Earlier in 1936, David Selznick had purchased the movie rights to Gone With the Wind for $50,000 prior to publication. As soon as Margaret Mitchell's Civil War novel became a best seller, the Selznick office started receiving thousands of letters and phone calls suggesting that Clark Gable play Rhett Butler. When Selznick approached him about it, Gable wanted no part of it. He said he wasn't good enough an actor to live up to the public's expectations.

Now that the book was such a phenomenal success, L. B. Mayer wanted *Gone With the Wind* for MGM and he offered Selznick a production setup similar to the one just vacated by Irving Thalberg. Still bristling over "the son-in-law also rises" jokes that circulated during his earlier employment at MGM, Selznick rejected Mayer's offer. He was now entrenched in his own company, Selznick International Pictures, which had the financial backing of John Hay Whitney and his family.

But Louis B. Mayer knew that if Selznick wanted Clark Gable for "Gone With the Wind," he would eventually have to reconsider the MGM offer.

Carole Lombard couldn't understand Gable's negative attitude about playing Rhett Butler. Not only could she visualize no one else in the part, but she could imagine no actress other than herself as Scarlett O'Hara, and she hoped that one day they could make the film together. Meanwhile, she was more interested in getting the role of Mrs. Clark Gable.

six

Echoes of Gable's Past

In late 1936, marriage seemed a long way off. With Gable still unable to face up to his wife's financial conditions for a divorce, Carole Lombard settled in for what she expected might be a lengthy term as his mistress. Selling her house on busy Hollywood Boulevard, she moved to the more secluded Bel-Air section, where Gable's arrivals and departures were less likely to be noticed. She christened her new home "The Farm," since it was styled after an English Tudor farmhouse.

Although he was virtually a permanent guest of Lombard's, Gable still maintained his rooms at the Beverly Wilshire Hotel for the sake of appearances, as he had been tipped off by mutual friends that his wife had hired private detectives to follow him, to try to catch him in a compromising situation with Lombard. So far, Gable hadn't noticed anyone shadowing them, but the lovers were being extra cautious.

Lombard had alerted her household staff to keep a lookout for any strangers lurking about. Between her three black servants, a cook, a butler, and a personal maid, and her noisy assortment of pets, Lombard figured that she had a very reliable alarm system. She later had the house completely fenced in and installed an electric gate to further protect their privacy.

Gable and Lombard also were forced to cut down on their public dating, since he did not want to antagonize his wife any more than was necessary. Jealous and resentful of Lombard, Mrs. Gable felt that she'd never been adequately compensated for all she had done to help her husband get established, and thought that she, rather than Lombard, should be sharing in his success. Whenever a picture of the lovers appeared in print, Mrs. Gable became more difficult and quarrelsome in her demands.

Lombard hated the crimp in her social life with Gable and frequently asked some of the eligible men she knew to take her out for an evening. This had disastrous results in the case of Anthony Quinn, then a struggling young actor playing a small role in Lombard's "Swing High, Swing Low." After Lombard made a date with him, he checked his low finances and ragged wardrobe and, realizing that he was in no position to escort anyone as stylish and important as Carole Lombard, he never showed up.

The next time that Lombard saw Quinn at the studio, she shouted, "You sonovabitch, you little shit, you bastard, you fucking little . . . I've never been stood up in my life before, you little prick." It was language like that which once earned Lombard an admonishment from a guide leading a studio sightseeing tour: "Please, Miss Lombard, there are ladies present." When she calmed down, Anthony Quinn explained his financial plight. Lombard was so moved that she was crying by the time he finished. Forgiving him, she said, "You're the only man that's ever stood me up and gotten away with it." She then did everything she could to further Quinn's career, finding him an agent and trying to persuade directors to use him in their new pictures. He was eventually signed to a Paramount contract, largely because of Lombard's efforts.

Shortly after the Quinn incident, Lombard was feeling so blue about her infrequent dates with Gable that she persuaded him to spend the 1936 Christmas-New Year's holiday with her in Sun Valley. They left town separately and returned separately. When there were no repercussions, Gable assumed that his wife's private detectives were either remiss or a figment of someone's vivid imagination.

Gable, then in the midst of filming "Parnell," based on the life of Charles Parnell, the "Uncrowned King of Ireland," was in a miserable frame of mind during production, as he detested working in historical pictures because he felt silly and uncomfortable in period dress. During the filming of Parnell's death scene, director John Stahl would play sad, funereal music on a phonograph to put Gable in the proper mood. By night, Gable was so depressed that Lombard couldn't stand being with him. She visited the set one morning to try to cheer him up, bribing a prop man to put a different record on the phonograph. When Stahl gave the signal to start the music, the jazzy "I'll Be Glad When You're Dead, You Rascal You" blasted through the air. Pandemonium followed, with Lombard making a hasty exit.

Lombard was usually in a playful mood with Gable, who delighted in her gags but rarely tried to get back at her for them. She was faster and cleverer than he and he knew that he couldn't top her. When he was invited to register his footprints and handprints in cement in the forecourt of Grauman's Chinese Theatre in January 1937, she teased him about it for days, telling him she'd arranged for the theater management to take him into their private office to make his "cockprint" as well. She also warned Gable that she was inviting Lee Francis, the leading madam in town, to bring a group of her fifty-dollar-a-night girls down to the ceremony to act as cheerleaders.

Before he fell in love with Lombard, Gable had been one of the madam's best customers. A friend once asked him why he paid a girl fifty dollars when so many other more desirable women could have been his for the asking. Gable answered, "Because with one of those floozies, I don't have to pretend that I'm Clark Gable."

Lombard didn't inject any of her pranks into the celebration of Gable's thirty-sixth birthday on February 1, since she didn't want to spoil the surprise already planned for him on the set of "Parnell." At the party, Gable discovered that he had a secret admirer, a chubby, giggly thirteen-year-old named Judy Garland, who climbed up on the refreshment table next to Gable's three-tiered birthday cake and sang special lyrics to the hit tune, "You Made Me Love You."

> *Dear Mr. Gable,*
> *I am writing this to you,*
> *And I hope that you will read it so you'll know.*
> *My heart beats like a hammer,*
> *And I stutter and I stammer,*
> *Everytime I see you at the picture show.*
> *I guess I'm just another fan of yours,*
> *And I thought I'd write and tell you so.*
> *You made me love you,*
> *I didn't want to do it,*
> *I didn't want to do it . . .*

Halfway through the number, Gable walked over and stood at Garland's feet so she could sing directly to him. When she finished, he lifted her down in his arms and kissed her. Garland was close to swooning as Gable whispered, "Thanks, honey, that was a real thrill." The MGM executives at the party were so impressed by Garland's performance that she was assigned to sing "Dear Mr. Gable" in "Broadway Melody of 1938." The scene was a show-stopper, starting Garland toward stardom at MGM.

Carole Lombard bought Garland's recording of "Dear Mr. Gable" and played it endlessly, driving its namesake, embarrassed and irritated by the song, to distraction. When Gable met Judy Garland at the studio one day, he embraced her and said, "Honey, I love you madly, but please don't do 'our song' any more." But the request was as futile as asking Al Jolson to never sing "Mammy" again. Garland was identified with "Dear Mr. Gable" and performed it for the rest of her life.

A few days after Gable's birthday, Carole Lombard received her first nomination for an Academy Award for "My Man Godfrey." She was thrilled because such an important honor confirmed the increasingly high opinion that Hollywood had of her talent.

Competing against Lombard for the best-actress Oscar were

Irene Dunne, Gladys George, Luise Rainer and Norma Shearer. Lombard desperately wanted the gold-plated statuette to put on her mantelpiece next to the one Gable had received for "It Happened One Night." She predicted, however, that, as an expression of the industry's respect for her recently deceased husband, Irving Thalberg, Norma Shearer would win.

The award went to Luise Rainer for "The Great Ziegfeld." Lombard was so disappointed that Gable tried to take the edge off her unhappiness by offering to have his own Oscar reinscribed to her.

But even a nomination for an Academy Award had value. This time it awakened the interest of David O. Selznick, who instructed his story department to start looking for a property that could be turned into a screwball comedy for Carole Lombard. They found one in a *Saturday Evening Post* story, which became the basis for a screenplay by Ben Hecht called "Nothing Sacred."

Lombard had always considered Selznick a producer of taste and integrity and was very enthusiastic when he approached her with the project. Despite her new contract with Paramount, she still didn't feel that the studio was handling her properly. After "The Princess Comes Across," she'd made another film with Fred Mac-Murray, "Swing High, Swing Low." While she and MacMurray were good friends, she didn't want to become fixed in the public's mind as part of a team, like Myrna Loy and William Powell, Jeanette MacDonald and Nelson Eddy or Fred Astaire and Ginger Rogers. She hoped that doing a picture for Selznick might change Paramount's attitude toward her.

Lombard also thought that if she ingratiated herself with Selznick, he might consider her for the role of Scarlett O'Hara in "Gone With the Wind." Miriam Hopkins, Tallulah Bankhead, Katharine Hepburn and Bette Davis were reported to being closest to getting the part, but since no one had definitely been signed, Lombard believed she still had a chance.

Gable immediately became suspicious when Lombard told him of her negotiations with Selznick that the producer might be using

Lombard as a means of persuading him to play Rhett Butler. Gable was still opposed to accepting the part and said that Ronald Colman should do it.

Lombard claimed that Gable was wrong about both Selznick and Colman, pointing out to Gable that she'd wanted him to play Rhett Butler ever since she'd read *Gone With the Wind*. Selznick didn't have to sign her to a contract to persuade her of something she already felt in her own heart.

Meanwhile, in the spring of 1937, Gable became the central figure in a blackmail scandal that, had it not been so ludicrous, might have ruined him. He had been receiving threatening letters on a fairly regular basis from a woman named Violet Norton, claiming that he was the father of her child. At first Gable thought the letters might be another of Carole Lombard's pranks. She often teased him about the rumors that he had a child by Loretta Young.

But soon a private detective representing Mrs. Norton turned up at MGM, demanding $150,000 for his client. If the studio wouldn't pay, Mrs. Norton threatened to reveal that Gable was really her ex-lover, Frank Billings, who had abandoned her after siring her thirteen-year-old daughter, Gwendoline. All this supposedly taken place in Mrs. Norton's native England.

MGM turned the case over to the United States Attorney General's office for investigation. When the story leaked out to the press, Gable's name was emblazoned in headlines across the country: "Mother Tells Gable to Confess"; "Is This Gable's Child?"; "Will Gable Come Clean?"; "Gable Paternity Mystery Rocks Hollywood."

The Hearst newspapers played the story up dramatically, with an anti-Gable slant. Some people thought it was William Randolph Hearst's way of getting back at Louis B. Mayer for MGM's maltreatment of Marion Davies. Mayer was so upset that he complained bitterly to the publisher, who said that if Gable could convince him of his innocence, he would call the papers off his neck. Hearst, then in residence at his castle in San Simeon, sent his private plane down to Los Angeles to bring Gable back for a private meeting.

The encounter was a success. The Hearst coverage of the case simmered down down after that, becoming decidedly favorable to Gable.

After studying all the evidence, the Federal Government indicted Violet Norton for using the mails to defraud. A trial was set for April, with Gable to be called as the key witness for the prosecution. Gable, who'd been treating it all pretty much as a joke, grew concerned. With his divorce settlement with Ria Gable still unresolved, even the remote possibility of another threat to his income and bank account was unsettling.

MGM's attorneys had located Mrs. Norton's daughter's birth certificate stating that she had been born in Essex, England, in 1923. If it could be established that Gable had never been in England, that he was somewhere else in the year preceding the child's birth, Mrs. Norton's charges would be proven fraudulent.

Gable was forced to recall a period in his life that he would rather have forgotten—his courtship of the young actress Frances Doerfler, who had since changed her name to Franz Dorfler and at one time was seeking a movie career. Gable ran into her in Hollywood from time to time, but hadn't seen her recently.

However, he told his attorneys that he had been keeping company with Dorfler around 1922–23, the period in question in the paternity case. He was sure that Dorfler, as well as her parents, would testify for him.

When asked what broke up his relationship with Dorfler, Gable said only that they had drifted apart. "After you threw her over?" one of the attorneys wanted to know. "What makes you think I threw her over?" Gable asked. "You must have," was the reply. "No one ever heard of a girl walking out on Clark Gable."

Gable, who wasn't about to reveal that he'd dropped Dorfler because she couldn't do as much for advancing his career as Josephine Dillon could at that time, didn't challenge that statement.

Gable said the last he'd seen Dorfler was about three years before, when she was on her way to an interview for a secretarial job at MGM. Asked if he'd offered to help her, Gable said it had never occurred to him. The lawyers wondered if he really thought Dorfler would want to testify in his behalf. Bewildered, Gable asked, "Why not?"

Gable also remembered the names of several other people he'd known in Oregon during that period, and a search was started to locate them. Franz Dorfler was found working as a kitchen helper. Before that, she'd been employed as a cook and a shop clerk. Her family had lost their farm early in the Depression and her father had died soon after.

Dorfler willingly agreed to testify in Gable's behalf. She seemed to bear no resentment over the fact that Gable had never done anything to assist her during her long period of bad luck, despite his own great success.

Louis B. Mayer, who was watching the case closely, thought it would make a better impression on the jury if Dorfler was introduced as an actress rather than a kitchen slavey, so MGM quickly signed her to a contract. It would also make her appear more glamorous and more worthy of Gable's attentions when the story of their romance came out in the course of the trial.

Carole Lombard thought that the Violet Norton case was the funniest thing that ever happened. She was always cutting out pictures of Mrs. Norton from the newspapers and hanging them over the bathroom mirror or under the lid of the toilet seat to tease Gable. When photographs of the alleged "love child" were published, Lombard held them up to Gable's face and pretended to find distinct resemblances around the eyes and ears.

But Lombard also saw a darker side to the case, which proved anew how careful celebrities like Gable and herself had to be in their private lives and how susceptible they were to blackmail and scandalmongering. She was also distressed by the revelations of Gable's behavior towards Franz Dorfler. For someone as generous and interested in other people as Lombard was, it was difficult to understand how Gable could treat his former girlfriend so shabbily. Lombard scolded him for it, but it was too late to do Dorfler any good.

Lombard was annoyed that she couldn't attend the trial. But that would have been the last thing Gable needed—having his mistress sitting in the front row and laughing while he was trying to prove himself innocent of yet another woman's paternity charges.

The trial started on April 20, 1937, before an all-male jury. Several prospective jurors were excused when they admitted they had already formed an opinion of Gable's character from his screen appearances. Another juror was exempted because he said he went to school with Jean Harlow's father.

Hundreds of women, most of them middle-aged or older, had started lining up the night before to gain admittance to the trial, and by morning, the line stretched completely around the courthouse. Inside, the corridors were filled with vendors hawking peanuts and souvenir photographs of Gable.

Gable did not get his first real look at Violet Norton until she entered the courtroom, a buxom, ruddy-faced woman of about fifty. When she spoke, she revealed a thick cockney accent and a cheap set of false teeth that rattled when she got excited.

Mae West, who'd received a letter from Mrs. Norton asking her to become the godmother of "Clark Gable's child," had been sought as a witness but managed to elude the subpoena servers. Columnist Jimmy Fidler described letters he'd received from Mrs. Norton as "the work of some kind of a nut." A representative of the Passport Office said that no passport had been issued to Gable, that would have made it possible for him to leave or reenter the country at that time. Four men who'd known Gable in Oregon testified to his whereabouts in the fall of 1922.

MGM went to work on Franz Dorfler before she was called to the witness stand, sending her to the beauty parlor for a permanent wave and a facial, and outfitting her in an expensive dress and picture hat. When her name was called, Gable bounded from his seat and escorted her to the witness chair.

Dorfler told of her early friendship with Gable, even intimating that they might have been married one day. When she was finished with her testimony, Gable again jumped up and led her by the arm back to her seat. He kissed her on the cheek and whispered his thanks. Many women in the audience were crying. It could have been a scene from a Gable movie, and, in fact, had been deliberately staged that way by his lawyers.

When Gable was called to testify, he confirmed all the facts stated by the previous witnesses. Mrs. Norton leaned forward as if she were hearing it all for the first time. As Gable finished, she shouted defiantly, "I still think Clark Gyble is the dad of me kid." Gable, unable to restrain himself, laughed out loud along with the rest of the spectators.

In her own testimony, Mrs. Norton said that Gable had seduced her while humming the tune of "I'm Forever Blowing Bubbles." She claimed she hadn't seen him until years later, when "I went to the pictures and there he was mykin' love to that Joan Crawford—just the syme as 'e did to me."

After deliberating for an hour and fifty-five minutes, the jury found Mrs. Norton guilty of using the mails to defraud, and she was sentenced to a year in jail. The following January, the woman and her daughter were deported to Canada, forbidden to ever return to the United States.

Gable and Lombard hadn't been out together publicly in weeks because of MGM's insistence that he try to avoid being linked with another woman while the Norton trial was going on. But right after it was over, they celebrated by going to William Randolph Hearst's seventy-fourth birthday party.

Hearst and Marion Davies threw a big costume extravaganza every year, each time with a different theme. The previous one, in 1936, had been a Spanish fiesta. This year it was the circus. Adjacent to Marion Davies' Santa Monica beach chateau, which was known as "The Social White House of Hollywood," Hearst had pitched a huge circus tent and inside he had installed the carousel featured in the Coney Island sequence in "Cain and Mabel." Hearst had lost three million dollars on that film, so he felt entitled to a little enjoyment for his money.

After going horseback riding that afternoon, Gable and Lombard decided to wear their same Western pants and shirts to the costume party, attending as a cowboy and cowgirl. Lombard bought them each new Stetsons and bandannas, white for herself and black for Gable. Instead of buying Hearst two separate birthday gifts, together they gave him a Shetland pony.

Five hundred guests were invited to the party. For those not arriving in costume, Hearst had set out racks and trunks filled with outfits rented from the Western Costume Company. Bette Davis at first refused to wear anything except the evening gown she'd arrived in. Later she relented, borrowing a pair of false whiskers and pretending she was the Bearded Lady. Cary Grant and his roommate, Randolph Scott, were a pair of tumblers in satin pantaloons. Ernst Lubitsch was a cigar-smoking Indian chief. Leslie Howard wore a black tuxedo and said he was a penguin. Anita Louise and Dolores Del Rio were tightrope walkers. Tyrone Power and ice-skating star Sonja Henie were polka-dotted clowns, Humphrey Bogart a hot-dog vendor. Louella Parsons and rival columnist Hedda Hopper were both dressed appropriately as lion tamers. And Marion Davies was a bareback rider, while Hearst wore a clown's suit but refused to put on greasepaint.

Gable didn't mix much at parties. At this one he was content just to sit at the table, ogling the other guests and Hearst's gigantic birthday cake, which this year resembled a multicolored circus tent. Lombard cuddled next to Gable, squeezing his arm. She was positive Ria Gable's detectives couldn't follow them there and she enjoyed showing off her man to all her friends.

But Lombard, who could never sit still for very long, was soon up, mingling and joking with the other guests. Gable stayed behind, looking slightly lost until Anita Louise sat down to chat.

Lombard ended up on the carousel, trying to catch the brass ring. Marion Davies had been after the same thing for most of the evening, but was too drunk to have any luck. When Davies finally grabbed one, she screamed even louder than she had when Gable and Lombard took her roller-coastering. Lombard almost fell off her horse as she joined in the applause for the hostess' success.

As the carousel was slowing down, Lombard suddenly noticed that Gable was dancing with Anita Louise. Lombard jumped down from her horse and was off the platform before it even stopped.

She stood watching Gable and his partner from the edge of the crowd.

One of the most beautiful blondes in Hollywood, Anita Louise had broken up a number of romances and marriages. She was rumored to have been the cause of at least two suicides, those of actor Ross Alexander and his jealous wife, Aleta Freel. Lombard didn't want Anita Louise, or any other woman, trying to take Gable away from her.

As soon as the dance was over, Lombard moved in and, taking Gable by the hand, led him back to their table, never letting him out of her sight the rest of the evening.

That Gable was now Lombard's exclusive property was further demonstrated a few weeks later when *Look* Magazine carried a feature article, "The Love Story of Clark Gable and Carole Lombard." It was the first time that a major national publication had taken notice of their romance, even though the article itself was somewhat of a tease. In eight pages there were only a few pictures of Gable and Lombard together. Most of the article rehashed their lives before they met. Lombard considered suing *Look* over one picture of herself, which showed the scar on her left cheek. Although that scar was almost undetectable now, she obviously still had a not-so-slight inner one.

The *Look* article went into little detail about Gable and Lombard's relationship but implied a great deal. A few days after the magazine hit the stands, Ria Gable demanded an immediate increase in her weekly payments. Gable complained that it would bankrupt him and the matter went to arbitration. Since their separation in late 1935, Gable had given his wife about $145,000, including two trust funds, in addition to half his salary. He would have to part with more than triple that before Mrs. Gable got her revenge on him and Carole Lombard.

seven

Sudden Tragedy

In the spring of 1937, Lombard teased Gable about his turning up second to nine-year-old Shirley Temple in the latest box-office popularity polls. Lombard advised Gable to drive over to 20th Century-Fox and put Shirley out of commission by spiking her orange juice with gin. Lombard's friend, W. C. Fields, had once done this to Baby LeRoy, putting him in a coma for thirty-six hours.

Though Lombard often sounded daffy, she really wasn't. As a friend once put it, "She was a lusty, rowdy, two-fisted, terrific dame, who knew all there was to know about life and love and temptation. Her philosophy was laughter. She had known black despair and heartbreak. She believed that you had to win through them and presume that good would triumph, and thus that laughter was an outward sign of an inward grace."

Up until now, Lombard was what Walter Winchell liked to call a "boudoir girl." When she wasn't working, she lounged around the house in a frilly negligee or tailored pajamas, buffing her nails and gossiping on the phone for hours at a time. Every night had to be a different party, premiere or nightclub.

For over a year, Gable and Lombard had been playing hard, almost exclusively her way. The initial excitement of such a life, which had been a novelty to Gable, began to pall on him. Basically a simple, unintellectual man, he felt most comfortable puttering around his cars or hunting and fishing. He started missing those activities and hinted to Lombard that she should try some of his favored pursuits.

Although she'd once told him that the outdoor life was for the birds and idiots, Lombard realized that developing interests closer to his was the key to holding Gable. Though a superb athlete in her younger days, shooting a gun and casting a fishing rod, however, still had to be learned.

Gable spent many free hours skeet shooting, and Lombard started tagging along with him whenever her schedule permitted. With practice, her rapid reflexes helped her to become a better shot than Gable. Her scores, using a 20-gauge Winchester rifle, were generally higher than his were with a 12-gauge pump gun, and she excelled in the "A" position, where she had no more than a fifth of a second to get her gun on her shoulder and fire. This was always Gable's worst position, for he was much heavier and less agile than Lombard. Among those giving her pointers in skeet shooting was a young athlete and aspiring actor named Robert Stack, who was the national 20-gauge champion in 1937 and also held a world's record of 354 straight hits. Lombard thought she was doing well if she hit 100.

Gable enjoyed fishing, but lacked the patience to teach Lombard how to fly-cast, so she learned largely by trial and error, in her own back yard. Her practice area was limited, however, and one day she invited herself over to Claudette Colbert's house, which had a huge sloping lawn. The two actresses spent a hectic afternoon with Colbert running about and unhooking Lombard's fishing line whenever it got snagged in the shrubbery.

One of Gable and Lombard's first outdoor excursions was to hunt ducks at a private club he belonged to near Bakersfield. By luck, Lombard hit a duck with her first shot. They had brought no dogs along, so Lombard acted as her own retriever, wading out in the water in Gable's hip boots to get the duck. Not knowing any better, she sloshed boldly forward, suddenly stepping into a rat hole and filling her boots with water. Certain that she was not in any danger, Gable stood on the shore laughing at her frantic efforts to pull herself out. In the meantime, the wind carried the duck too far away to ever be retrieved.

When she finally worked herself out of the boots and waded back through the cold water in her bare feet, Lombard was fuming. "I'll show you up yet," she threatened Gable, as she pulled off her soaking-wet pants and hurled them at him. "No fucking duck can get the best of me."

Gable was working then in "Saratoga," his sixth picture with Jean Harlow. The platinum blonde had been in failing health for several months and should have been resting. She was rushed into the film after Joan Crawford turned down the role. Harlow, though complaining of headaches and dizziness, gallantly tried to carry on. She had recently celebrated the third anniversary of her affair with Lombard's ex-husband, William Powell, who had gifted her with a one-hundred-and-fifty-carat star sapphire ring.

Gable's love scenes with Jean Harlow were always sexier than those he played with any other actress. Harlow urged him on in a way that no one else would have dared, though she did it all in fun. Except on the day she was introduced to President Roosevelt, Harlow never wore any underclothes. She took great joy in her body and loved to thrust herself at Gable with all the strength she could muster. This never failed to arouse Gable, causing him to respond in an equally abandoned way.

On May 29, Gable and Harlow were filming a bedroom scene for "Saratoga" in which Gable was supposed to sweep Harlow up in his arms and then throw her down on a chaise longue.

As soon as Gable picked Harlow up, he realized that something was wrong with her. Her body felt limp, her brow was beaded with sweat. Signaling to director Jack Conway to stop the scene, Gable gently lowered Harlow onto the chaise. She started to get up, then mumbled that she felt sick and collapsed. An assistant director revived her with smelling salts and carried her to her dressing room, but Harlow was too sick to continue. She was taken home in a private car to avoid the attention that an ambulance would have attracted.

The filming of "Saratoga" continued without Harlow for a few days, concentrating on scenes in which she didn't appear. Whenever Gable or Lombard phoned to check on Harlow's condition, her mother would tell them only that the patient was better and that she would be back to work soon.

But when Harlow didn't return the following week, Gable, together with Jack Conway and actor Frank Morgan, drove to her house. Harlow's mother met Gable and his friends at the door but refused to let them enter. Forcing their way in, they found Harlow semiconscious in bed, belching and moaning about severe pains in her stomach. Despite the protests of her mother, a Christian Scientist who believed that prayer alone would cure her daughter, Harlow was rushed by ambulance to Good Samaritan Hospital.

When Gable described the events to Lombard, she was shocked that MGM had allowed Harlow to remain unattended for so long. It seemed incredible to both Gable and Lombard that Louis B. Mayer, usually so paternal toward his female stars, had not intervened. The incident started all kinds of rumors, the most persistent being that Mayer had once tried unsuccessfully to make Harlow his mistress, and that by ignoring her illness he was getting even with her for spurning him.

Despite Harlow's worsening condition, her mother refused to permit an operation. On June 7, Harlow developed breathing difficulties. The hospital sent an emergency call to the Fire Department Inhalator Squad for help, but it was too late. She died a few minutes later.

The news of Harlow's death spread so quickly that Carole Lombard told Gable that the Associated Press must have secretly taped a wire to the actress' wrist so they'd know the moment her pulse stopped. Not since Rudolph Valentino died of a perforated ulcer in 1926 had one of Hollywood's great sex symbols succumbed at the height of fame and popularity. With eighty-eight million Americans worshipping in movie cathedrals every week, it was a tragedy epic enough to sweep even the honeymoon of the Duke and Duchess of Windsor out of the headlines.

Louis B. Mayer announced that out of respect to Harlow's memory, "Saratoga" was being abandoned, at a loss to MGM of half a million dollars. He neglected to say that most of that sum was covered by insurance. Little work was accomplished on the five other pictures shooting at MGM that day. The switchboard operators were crying as they answered the studio phones.

Many of the callers wanted to know what had killed Jean Harlow. The official answer was a cerebral edema or swelling of the brain, induced by an infected kidney. But since MGM was notorious for trying to manage the news, many people refused to believe that simple explanation, some suspecting that Harlow had died as the result of a botched abortion, others that heavy drinking had ruined her kidneys. There was another theory that the kidney damage dated back to a savage caning at the hands of her second husband, the impotent Paul Bern, who compensated for his sexual inadequacies by beating his wife. Bern died shortly after their marriage, apparently by suicide, and Harlow took the secret of that episode with her to the grave.

Gable and Lombard were badly shaken by Harlow's death. Though she was generally known around the studio as "The Baby," Gable called Harlow "Sis" and they had been very close since their early days at MGM. Harlow reminded Gable of Lombard in some ways. Both were ribald and fun-loving, greatly admired by their co-workers for their friendliness and unpretentiousness. Gable could clown and wisecrack with Harlow as freely as he could with Lombard.

Lombard, who at twenty-eight was two years older than Harlow, again sensed something of her own mortality in Harlow's death. They both had their early training in silent two-reel comedies and had achieved stardom around the same time. Both had a lusty, open attitude toward love and sex. Lombard had been somewhat envious of Harlow's relationship with William Powell, though it was not because he was her former husband. Rather, since both Harlow and Powell were single, they could flaunt their romance much more openly than Lombard could with her still-married lover.

Gable and Lombard drove to the Pierce Brothers Mortuary to pay their respects to William Powell and Harlow's mother and stepfather. Members of the MGM police force directed them to the Alfred Tennyson Room, where Harlow's body reposed on a couch under a portrait of the poet.

"Christ, she looks so terrific she'd probably sit up and shake my hand if I tapped her on the shoulder," someone whispered in the line ahead of Gable and Lombard. Together with the mortuary's cosmetician, a makeup artist and hairdresser from MGM had worked all through the night on Harlow's body so that it would show none of the ravages of her illness. A faint smile was now frozen on her lips. Harlow's famous blond hair, which had been softened from platinum to a honey shade for "Saratoga," cascaded luxuriantly about her face and shoulders. Actually, it was a wig. Harlow's own hair had been so ruined by overbleaching that she always wore a wig in her films and public appearances.

Gable, who had been the last man to hold Harlow in his arms, had tears in his eyes as he passed the body. Lombard, too, was crying. William Powell, wearing smoked glasses, was sobbing, "I don't know how I'll go on without my baby." Lombard promised to lend him her secretary, Fieldsie, to help him straighten out business details. Ronald Colman, another friend, offered Powell the use of his yacht for a rest cruise.

As they left the mortuary, Gable pointed out to Lombard that the building seemed to be completely surrounded by many of the prop men, electricians, messengers and other workers he knew from MGM. One of them told Gable that they would be on guard all night: "The baby didn't like to be alone in the dark."

Gable was selected to serve as a pallbearer and usher at Harlow's funeral. MGM, which had a habit of controlling its stars' lives right up to the grave, was planning the rites as a superproduction rivaling any of its pictures. The setting was Forest Lawn Memorial Park, the Valhalla of such Hollywood immortals as Marie Dressler, Will Rogers, Lon Chaney, Wallace Reid, Irving Thalberg and Alexander Pantages, as well as Broadway's Florenz Ziegfeld. Fearing a repercussion of the frenzied rioting that had been touched off at Rudolph Valentino's funeral, the entire MGM, Forest Lawn and Glendale police departments were ordered to be on hand to keep the crowds under control and discreetly out of sight of the two hundred invited celebrities.

Lombard's mourning ensemble was a simple black silk dress and black Persian lamb cape; her blond hair was piled up beneath a black turban. She hoped no one would notice that she'd worn the same dress to Irving Thalberg's funeral. Gable wore a single-breasted black serge suit.

When Gable and Lombard entered the two-hundred-acre cemetery, a large crowd of sightseers had gathered at the main gate. An MGM police officer saluted Gable and asked him to stop his car so the trunk could be searched for stowaways. Gable then stepped on the gas and raced through the burial grounds known as Babyland, Slumberland and the Vale of Memory. His destination was the Wee Kirk on the Heather, a replica of the old Scottish church where Annie Laurie worshipped, and the only church in Forest Lawn used exclusively for funerals. The larger Little Church of the Flowers was frequently the site of happier events, such as the wedding of Ginger Rogers and Lew Ayres.

Gable ushered Lombard to a place near the back of the chapel of the Wee Kirk so that he could sit with her once all the guests had been ushered in. Harlow's copper coffin was closed and covered with a huge blanket of her favorite white gardenias and 1,500 lilies of the valley. Lombard had sent a wreath of white carnations, larkspur and blue delphiniums; Gable's tribute was a wreath of white roses, gardenias and gladioluses.

Gable conducted Harlow's first and third husbands, Charles McGrew and Hal Rosson, to front-row seats next to her father and stepfather. Harlow's mother and William Powell were seated in a private alcove off to one side, away from the other mourners.

Within a few minutes, the chapel was filled with movie stars, studio executives and reporters. The audience was a "Who's Who in Hollywood," with Greta Garbo the only notable absentee.

Just as the service started, Gable squeezed into the seat Lombard had been holding for him. Jeanette MacDonald sang one of Harlow's favorite songs, "Indian Love Call." A Christian Science practitioner, the same one who advised Harlow's mother not to seek medical help for her daughter, read from the Bible and *Science and Health,* then recited a short eulogy and the Lord's Prayer.

Lombard started to cry and covered her face with her hands. His head bowed, Gable tried to comfort her. But he was suddenly forced to lurch from his seat as Barbara Browne, Harlow's stand-in, became hysterical and had to be ushered from the church.

The twenty-three-minute service ended with Jeanette Mac-Donald and Nelson Eddy singing "Ah, Sweet Mystery of Life." MacDonald broke down in tears in the middle of the song, forcing Eddy to finish it alone. When an airplane dropping white gardenias droned noisily overhead, momentarily drowning out Eddy's baritone, a reporter near Lombard cracked, "If that plane comes much closer, they won't ever have to hold another funeral in this town."

Gable looked grim as he helped to lift the heavy coffin into the hearse. As soon as William Powell and Harlow's relatives drove off to tuck their baby away in a $25,000 vault in the Romanesque Sanctuary of Benediction, the mourners quickly departed in their limousines and sports cars. Within minutes, sightseers invaded the Wee Kirk and stripped bare the $15,000 worth of floral tributes.

Gable and Lombard both hated the irreverent spectacle and tasteless impersonality of such affairs, which were almost automatic for any important person in Hollywood. Lombard told Gable that she was going to have it written into her will that when she died, her funeral was to be private, with only her family and a few intimate friends invited. Gable, already overburdened by sadness and grief, quickly made her change the subject.

Not long after the funeral, Louis B. Mayer announced that "Saratoga" would be released after all, claiming that Harlow had finished all of her important scenes before she died. In response to what Mayer termed "overwhelming popular demand," the film was to be completed and released as soon as possible. But the real reason was greed. MGM knew that the publicity over Harlow's death would earn her last picture a fortune.

Someone at the studio had remembered that Harlow once had a stand-in, Mary Dees, who looked enough like the star to be her twin sister. Though she would get no screen credit, Mary Dees was hired to play Harlow's remaining scenes, more numerous than MGM had been willing to admit. These scenes were cleverly rewritten so that Mary Dees was always photographed at odd angles, with her back to the camera or with a big hat largely obscuring her face. Mary Dees' voice, however, had none of Jean Harlow's brassy shrillness, and her dialogue had to be dubbed in by still another actress.

After the first day of the renewed shooting of "Saratoga," Gable was visibly shaken. "I feel like I've been holding a ghost in my arms all day," he complained to Lombard.

Gable finished "Saratoga" on June 29 and MGM released it three weeks later. While not as good a film as some of Gable and Harlow's earlier ones together, it was very successful, giving Gable's popularity a needed boost after "Parnell," which had been Gable's first box-office disaster for MGM. He told Lombard he would never attempt another historical picture, that he was more determined than ever not to play Rhett Butler.

MGM had recently opened a new studio in England and wanted to send Gable over to make a film called "Shadow of the Wing." For one of the few times in his career, Gable balked at the studio's plans for him. Since he knew it would be impossible for Lombard to accompany him, he couldn't face being without her for an extended period of time.

This left Gable with several months free while MGM prepared another picture for him, and one of the first things he did to pass the time was to repair the old Valentine's Day Ford that Lombard had given him. He souped up the car with an overhead valve engine that could reach a top speed of 125 miles per hour. The first time he took Lombard out for a drive, she was so frightened that she refused to ride in it again. Gable surprised her by buying a rubber-tired sulky, which was more Lombard's speed. On her day off, they'd rent a horse to hitch to the sulky and go racing up and down the San Fernando Valley.

Lombard had started making "Nothing Sacred." She was earning $18,750 a week, which is what her $150,000 fee broke down to over the eight-week shooting schedule. She felt she deserved this fee, because "Nothing Sacred" was more strenuous and exhausting than any film she'd ever made. She was playing Hazel Flagg, a small-town girl who becomes a national celebrity when she's mistakenly diagnosed as dying of radium poisoning. After one scene in which she'd been swinging punches and wrestling with Fredric March, she was so bruised and scratched she had to be given the next day off.

But the hardest part of the picture for Lombard were her love scenes with Fredric March, who was not one of her favorites. A great ladies' man, March had once made a play for Lombard when they were both under contract to Paramount. Lombard didn't fancy March's attentions and pulled one of her raunchiest pranks to discourage him. Inviting March to her dressing room for a drink one night, she proceeded to make herself available. As March's hand started up under Lombard's dress, he suddenly let out an astonished oath. He had grabbed a rubber dildo, which Lombard had strapped on herself before his arrival. The shock was too much for March. He never bothered Lombard again.

In order to get Lombard into the proper mood for her scenes with March in "Nothing Sacred," director William Wellman would shout at her, "Miss Lombard, I know it must be tough to look into Freddie's frozen puss and pretend to be in love with him. But close your eyes or something and let's try it."

Lombard hated being called "Miss," a form of address generally reserved for the most spoiled and temperamental stars. She'd scream "Fuck off" or "Shit" at Wellman before puckering up and giving Fredric March whatever the script called for. Lombard got even with the director at the end of the filming by tying him up in a straitjacket with the help of a few technicians.

Gable wanted to take Lombard on a hunting trip to Mexico as soon as she finished "Nothing Sacred," but she owed Paramount a picture and had to report to them almost immediately. She was again teamed with Fred MacMurray, this time in a nutty comedy called "True Confession," in which she played a perpetual liar who confesses to a murder she didn't commit in order to create work for her lawyer husband.

Gable was getting restless at seeing so little of Lombard while she was working. When filming of "True Confession" moved to Lake Arrowhead for the climactic motorboat chase, Lombard invited Gable to come along and spend a few days with her. They managed to find enough free time for swimming and horseback riding, and, while there, also celebrated Lombard's twenty-ninth birthday.

Gable and Lombard's brief idyll together did not go unnoticed by Ria Gable, who now had private detectives on his trail twenty-four hours a day. His wife still hadn't been able to establish sufficient evidence for a divorce action, but Gable had been informed that she was more incensed than ever over his liaison with Lombard.

Mrs. Gable didn't know it, but she and Carole Lombard had the same manicurist, Peggy Mercer, at Ann Meredith's Beauty Salon in Beverly Hills. Whenever Lombard had her nails done, she heard the latest bitchy remarks that her lover's jealous wife had made about her. Mrs. Gable's constant references to Lombard as a home-breaker especially annoyed Lombard, who had not become involved with Gable until long after he left his wife.

Lombard decided to teach Ria Gable a lesson. Late one night, she drove out alone to Mrs. Gable's house in Brentwood and climbed through a window. There was no one about, but Lombard noticed a light at the top of the stairs. Tiptoeing upstairs, she found Ria Gable reading in bed.

Lombard padded quietly to the doorway, cleared her throat and yelled at the startled Mrs. Gable, "Hi, you old witch. If you want to call me a home-breaker now, it's your fucking privilege." Without giving Mrs. Gable time to answer, Lombard ran down the stairs and out the front door. Later, she told Gable she was laughing so hard that she almost drove her car off Sunset Boulevard into a tree.

But there was also a more serious side to Gable and Lombard's lives at that time. William Powell was gravely ill, and now that Jean Harlow had died, Lombard and her friend Fieldsie were the only ones to look after him. Powell had rectal cancer, and he underwent a colon bypass operation and radiation treatments. Lombard and Fieldsie nursed Powell through his illness, which MGM diagnosed as "eye trouble" when it announced the actor's temporary retirement from the screen.

Not long after that, Gable's writer friend Donald Ogden Stewart was run down by a truck while crossing Hollywood Boulevard. Now separated from his wife, Stewart had no place to go when he was released from the hospital, so Lombard invited him to stay at her house, where she and Gable took care of him for a week while he recuperated. Stewart thought this a very courageous gesture on their part. He had become quite unpopular in Hollywood because of his interest in communism and his participation in antifascist activities. Gable and Lombard were risking censure by the industry for taking Stewart in, but their friend's well-being seemed to be more important to them than public opinion.

eight

A Wife in All But Name

"Can the Gable-Lombard Love Story Have a Happy Ending?" was more than a fan magazine headline in the early part of 1938. As the relationship entered its third year, no one seemed to know the answer. Rather accurately, one observer predicted that "time will furnish its climax and its end. It may be one of the deepest tragedies or one of the most poignant romances of Hollywood." It turned out to be both.

For all practical purposes, Lombard had turned herself into Gable's wife, even though she didn't yet have his name. Their affair, hardly one of Hollywood's best-kept secrets, was tolerated because Gable and Lombard were so well liked and seemed such a perfect match. Everyone, press and public alike, relished such a real-life fairytale romance, and opinion was all on the side of the lovers. Every move that Ria Gable made against them only strengthened that sympathetic attitude. Mrs. Gable had clung so long and bargained so hard that only the most hard-nosed moralists could have found anything wrong with the private, unobtrusive way that Gable and Lombard conducted their life together.

The Gable-Lombard relationship was becoming noteworthy for the effect they were having on each other's personalities. His association with Lombard was adding an extra dimension to Gable, increasing his self-confidence and making him into the strong, dominant male his two wives had never permitted him to be. Before he met Lombard, he had been coasting along in the stuffy, soporific atmosphere that Ria Gable had created. He shed years, visibly, with Lombard.

On the other hand, Gable was taming Lombard down, taking some of the hoyden out of her. She seemed more mature, with a new kind of gaiety about her. She no longer needed laughs, she just enjoyed them. She was no longer straining to call attention to herself, nor was she afraid of failure. She was simply in love, beloved and quietly sure of herself. Not that she stopped being the prankster; laughter was a deeply essential part of Carole Lombard and always would be.

Gable was becoming tired of sneaking in and out of Lombard's Bel-Air home at odd hours of the day and night, disrupting the household and putting a strain on her family, friends and servants. He rented a small house in Laurel Canyon as a hideaway for the two of them, but his wife found out about it and he was forced to give it up. Later, he moved out of his rooms at the Beverly Wilshire and leased the former home of director Rex Ingram and actress Alice Terry in North Hollywood. Gable's wife couldn't object to that setup, since he was entitled to a roof over his head. But Lombard still had to be very careful about the time she spent there with Gable.

Lombard loved Gable very much, but there were moments when she wondered whether he felt that deeply about her. She thought that if he was really sincere, he should have divorced his wife by now, regardless of the cost.

She had little to worry about as far as his affection for her was concerned. Gable often boasted to his close friends that there wasn't anybody like her, that he would rather spend the rest of his life with Lombard than with anybody he ever knew. "You can trust that little screwball with your life or your hopes or your weaknesses and she wouldn't even know how to think about letting you down," Gable once said. "She's more fun than anybody, but she'll take a poke at you if you have it coming and make you like it. If that adds up to love, then I love her."

The reason why Gable was taking so long about his divorce was that he couldn't reconcile himself to making the financial sacrifice. Despite his success, he was driven by great feelings of insecurity, never forgetting the deprivations and hard times of his first thirty years. Afraid that his luck wouldn't hold, he often talked of eventually going back to some kind of manual labor, as a farmer or a garage mechanic. Consequently Gable was very miserly. Whatever he managed to save—and his weekly payments to his wife didn't leave him with a great deal—he hoarded in cash in a safety-deposit box. He had no investments in stock, real estate or other enterprises that involved any risk. He liked his money where he could put his hands on it quickly, and he always carried several thousand dollars in his wallet.

Lombard found this side of Gable hard to understand, because she was just the opposite when it came to money, spending lavishly, and her generosity was legendary in Hollywood. At the studio she was always good for a touch, and she often took the initiative, seeking out people who had problems and paying their bills without any thought of ever being reimbursed. She also contributed to many charities, especially one that Hollywood pretended did not exist—a home and hospital for unwed mothers who were actresses or employees of the industry.

The Gable-Lombard affair achieved royal status in February 1938, when Gable was officially elected "The King of Hollywood." More than twenty million votes were cast in a public contest conducted by Ed Sullivan, movie columnist for the Chicago Tribune-New York Daily News Syndicate. The "Queen" was Myrna Loy, who was working opposite Gable in "Test Pilot" at the time. Their crowns, made of tin and purple velvet, were presented to them in a national coronation broadcast on NBC.

"King" was linked with Gable's name for the rest of his life. Lombard was proud of the new title, since she felt it honestly reflected the public's affection and admiration for him. Though she kidded Gable about it from time to time, especially at moments when she thought he was getting too chesty, she never used "King" as a nickname for him, as she did "Pa," "Pappy" or "Moose."

Lombard's favorite method of deflating Gable, though, was to mention his great flop, "Parnell." When he started bragging about his performance in "Test Pilot," Lombard had leaflets printed that read: "If you think Gable is the world's greatest actor, see him in 'Parnell.' You'll never forget it. If Parnell was as woozy a goof as Gable portrayed him in that picture, Ireland still wouldn't be free." Lombard tried to rent a plane to drop the leaflets from the sky over MGM, but when she couldn't get the necessary clearance, she instead hired some actors from Central Casting to distribute the leaflets at the studio's main entrance.

Lombard had acquired a title of her own by the time Gable became "The King." Critics liked her performances in "Nothing Sacred" and "True Confession" so much that she was being dubbed "The Screwball Queen of the Screen." "Nothing Sacred" was a smash hit. Together with Lombard's "My Man Godfrey" and Gable's "It Happened One Night," it was one of the three most famous zany comedies of the Thirties.

"True Confession" suffered by being released only a week after "Nothing Sacred," putting Lombard in the unenviable position of competing against herself, with the better picture winning. This was the last straw as far as Paramount's mishandling of her career was concerned. She thought she could do much better freelancing. Since she had script approval, she rejected all of the projects Paramount submitted to her for the balance of her contract and she never made another picture for that studio.

Lombard took her time about making a new outside deal. In 1937 she had earned $465,000, making her the highest-paid star in Hollywood. Once again, she had proven herself a winner. She could afford to take life a little easier and spend more time with Gable.

Gable didn't have that much time for Lombard while he was making "Test Pilot," the most ambitious aviation picture filmed in

Hollywood since "Hell's Angels." Many of the outdoor scenes were being photographed at March Field, near Riverside, California, with eighteen cameras and as many as a hundred planes in the sky at one time.

A great rivalry was developing between Gable and Spencer Tracy, who in "Test Pilot" was again teamed with him. Tracy, who had just achieved a major success in "Captains Courageous" and resented being reduced to playing Gable's sidekick, compensated by trying to steal every scene he could from Gable. But Gable didn't care, since he thought Tracy was the greatest actor in the world.

Gable was much better liked around the set than Tracy, who tended to lose his violent Irish temper at the least provocation. One morning Tracy turned up nursing a bad hangover, his face looking very tired, his hair a mess. The makeup man tried to fix him up before he went in front of the cameras, but Tracy told him to go away. Later, after Tracy had seen the rushes, he berated the makeup man: "Why the hell can't you make me look as good as Gable?"

In the crowded officers' mess at March Field one night, Gable and director Victor Fleming persuaded a pilot to take them up in one of the new B-17 flying fortresses that were being used in the film. Spencer Tracy wanted to join them, but he had been drinking heavily. Afraid that he might suddenly go berserk in the plane, Gable and Fleming told Tracy he must stay behind. Tracy was so embarrassed by being turned down in front of all the Army officers in the room that he went off by himself on a drinking spree. He didn't show up for work the next day; he remained missing for twenty-four hours.

Gable was eager to go hunting after "Test Pilot" was finished, and he persuaded Lombard to accompany him. They decided to spend a few days at Gable's gun club near Bakersfield but there was one hitch: a woman had never stayed overnight at the all-male preserve.

She solved the problem of accommodations by buying herself a small trailer, complete with kitchen and bathroom, as she had no intention of sharing the men's outdoor privy. Since the sight of Gable and Lombard pulling a trailer together down the main highway would have upped Ria Gable's divorce demands by thousands of dollars, Lombard had to haul the trailer out to the club by herself, parking about fifty feet from the shack that served as the men's sleeping quarters.

Gable and Lombard spent most of the day hunting by themselves. When they returned to camp at night, the men—about twenty of them—were sitting around drinking, telling off-color jokes and playing poker. They did not seem pleased about having a woman in their midst, and they mumbled and grumbled among themselves until Lombard finally got the message and retreated to her trailer.

An hour later, the smell of freshly baked bread and the tinkle of ice cubes started emanating from Lombard's trailer. Within minutes, every man in the camp was at her door. A party was soon in progress, and she had to send Gable out for more liquor.

When bedtime came, the men started teasing Gable about where he was going to sleep that night. Lombard made it quite clear that it wasn't going to be with her. She said, "Goodnight, boys, it's been swell" and shooed them away, Gable included. Her only companion that night was Pushface, her Pekingese.

Gradually, Lombard so endeared herself to the members of the club that she became the only woman to be admitted there on a regular basis. She never demanded special consideration because she was a woman. She did whatever was expected of everyone else, whether it was lying flat on her stomach with her face in the mud or lugging twenty-five pounds of guns and equipment on her back. It was quite a change for one of the most glamorous women in the world, but she seemed to enjoy it.

Though the outdoor life with Gable was becoming more and more attractive to Lombard, she still could not lose sight of her career. "Fools for Scandal," another comedy she'd made right after "Nothing Sacred" and "True Confession," proved a critical and box-office disaster. While Lombard realized that a poor script was largely the reason for the film's failure, she wondered if the public wasn't beginning to lose its appetite for screwball comedies. In the past year alone, twenty-three had been released, with everyone from Irene Dunne to Katharine Hepburn trying to prove that they could be as goofy as Carole Lombard.

Lombard thought it was time to change her screen image again. Now that she had proved she had no equal as a comedienne, the next logical move was toward more serious dramatic roles. After the success of "Nothing Sacred," David Selznick had offered her a contract for two more pictures. Lombard accepted, provided that the first picture allowed her to go dramatic. Though she didn't mention it to Selznick, she still had hopes of playing Scarlett O'Hara and thought that if she could demonstrate her dramatic abilities to him, he would have to give her more serious consideration for the part.

It now looked as if Gable would be Selznick's Rhett Butler, whether he liked it or not. Selznick was negotiating seriously with Louis B. Mayer, and in August 1938, they announced that MGM would release "Gone With the Wind" and receive 50 percent of the profits, in exchange for Clark Gable's services and $1,250,000 in financial backing.

Gable grumbled for weeks, telling Lombard he felt as if he'd been sold down the river. The slave auctioneer, Louis B. Mayer, had Gable backed into a corner. If Gable refused to do "Gone With the Wind," MGM would suspend him without pay, a situation Mayer knew that Gable could not afford because of his present and future financial obligations to his wife. Mayer did everything he could to make Gable aware of his untenable position. A close friend of Mrs. Gable's attorney, Mayer was pretending to be very sympathetic to her cause, hoping to keep her provoked and on her husband's neck at all times.

Lombard's new picture for Selznick was "Made for Each Other." The producer borrowed James Stewart from MGM to play her husband in the romantic drama, which depicted the problems of a young couple in the first year of their marriage. Selznick's publicity chief, Russell Birdwell, did not lose sight of Lombard's screwball side. He talked the authorities of Culver City into declaring "Carole Lombard Day" and appointing her honorary mayor. Her first official act was to declare a studio holiday and dismiss all employees for the balance of the day, much to Selznick's displeasure.

Birdwell engineered another stunt that made Lombard somewhat of a national heroine. Irritated by a studio executive's constant complaints about the astronomical income tax he had to pay, Lombard told Birdwell that she was proud to pay taxes because they contributed to the national welfare. At that time, when the United States was still feeling its way out of the Depression, people with low incomes were annoyed when the wealthy complained about overtaxation. Lombard's coming out in favor of the income-tax system was a startling stand for the highest-salaried star in Hollywood.

At Birdwell's prompting, Lombard called the major news services and gave them her story, which drew headlines like "Carole Lombard Is Glad U.S. Takes Most of Pay." She revealed that out of her earnings of $465,000 in 1937, she paid $285,000 to the Federal Government and $54,000 to the state. After business deductions and other expenses, she ended up with only about $50,000 for herself. She said, "The Government spent what they took from my earnings in general improvements for the country, and I really think I got my money's worth." Lombard won many admirers for that statement, including President Roosevelt, who sent her a personal note of thanks.

When Lombard was playing a screwball part, she carried the role home with her, much to Gable's distress. When she was playing a young mother whose baby is critically ill in "Made for Each Other," she became so emotionally involved in the story that she would come home from the studio at night and cry for hours. She couldn't even talk to Gable without choking up.

But she could still find time for a prank. Gable was starting an adventure melodrama with Myrna Loy, about a newsreel cameraman and a lady aviator entitled "Too Hot to Handle." On the first day of shooting, Lombard sent Gable a cardboard box labeled "Too Hot to Handle." Inside were a pair of asbestos gloves and an envelope filled with pornographic pictures.

One night Gable came home with a story which did not amuse Lombard very much, since it involved another woman. Two of his friends among the technical crew had brought a young call girl to the set, introduced her to Gable as a starstruck teen-ager who was dying to meet him, and talked him into inviting the girl into his dressing room for lunch. As soon as they were alone, the girl proved much less innocent than she appeared. She threw herself at Gable, unbuttoned the fly of his trousers and exposed him. "You ain't got much, have you?" she said, giggling, and ran out of the room. Gable was so dumbfounded that he was still unbuttoned when his friends returned to tell him it was all a joke.

Though Lombard warned him to be wary of such friends, Gable laughed about the incident. He enjoyed the company of the men he worked with and was intensely loyal to them. When an electrician friend developed a crush on a pretty bit player in "Too Hot to Handle," Gable let them use his dressing room as a trysting place. Ida Koverman, L. B. Mayer's snoop-nosed secretary, found out about it and had the electrician fired. When Gable then called Koverman on the phone and told her, "My boys can do anything they want in my dressing room," the dismissal notice was immediately rescinded.

MGM starred Gable in three films in 1938, since the studio knew that once he started "Gone With the Wind" for Selznick he would be unavailable to them for many months. Shortly after "Too Hot to Handle" was finished, Gable made "Idiot's Delight" with Norma Shearer. Shearer's popularity was waning and Louis B. Mayer had hoped that "Gone With the Wind" would revitalize her career. But fan-mail reaction to her proposed role as Scarlett O'Hara had been so adverse that she dropped out of the race. To make it up to her, Mayer promised Shearer she could have Gable as her leading man in "Idiot's Delight."

Carole Lombard had never forgiven Shearer for turning up in that red dress at The White Mayfair. When she heard that Gable

was being teamed with Shearer, Lombard sensed another contre-
temps brewing. Now that her mourning period for Irving Thalberg
was over, Shearer was known around Hollywood as the Merry
Widow. Her steady companion was George Raft, but she was also
dating others as well.

It was obvious to some people working on "Idiot's Delight"
that Shearer was pursuing Gable. At one point Gable got so fed up
with the situation that he told a photographer, "I wish this broad
would get the hell out of here." Shearer might not have been
Gable's type, but a more urgent reason for his keeping his distance
was that he feared Lombard's censure.

Certain that the problems with Ria Gable would eventually
be resolved and that they would be free to marry, Lombard started
shopping around for a house for the two of them as soon as she
finished "Made for Each Other." For a time she had considered
their keeping her place in Bel-Air as their home, but Gable
thought it was too small; he had always dreamed of having a farm
or a ranch, where he could indulge his love for the outdoors, maintain a stable of horses and perhaps even raise a few crops and
livestock. This wasn't exactly Lombard's idea of paradise, but she
was determined to do anything that she thought would make Gable
happy.

Lombard followed up dozens of leads from real estate agents
and newspaper ads, but wasn't very enthusiastic about any of them
until she heard that director Raoul Walsh's twenty-acre ranch in
Encino, in the San Fernando Valley, was on the market. Lombard
had known the director since her Pathé days. She and Gable had
visited the ranch several times and were impressed by its beautiful
rural setting. For all its trees and rolling hills, it had the added
attraction of being no more than forty-five minutes by car from
any of the major movie studios.

Gable and Lombard looked the place over on one of his days
off from "Idiot's Delight." Gable liked the main house because it
looked more Eastern than most he'd seen in California. It was a
two-story Connecticut farmhouse, built only thirteen years before
but artificially weatherbeaten to appear much older. The ranch had

several smaller buildings including a stable, a barn, a workshop and a garage.

Lombard ran around the grounds trying to count the trees, but there were too many—pepper, eucalyptus, avocado, plum, peach, apricot and fig. A separate citrus orchard was filled with orange, lemon and grapefruit trees.

When Gable and Lombard went to look over the interior of the house, she proved once again how much she'd changed since he first met her. Who would have expected the madcap Carole Lombard to take a folding ruler out of her handbag and start measuring space in the kitchen for a new refrigerator? Much to Gable's surprise and amusement, she then checked all the plumbing, making sure that the water pressure was adequate and that the toilets flushed properly and even examining all the wall beams and moldings for termites.

Lombard dragged Gable about the house, pointing out all the changes she would want to make and describing how the house would look afterward. Gable never had to say he wanted the ranch; Lombard had already made up his mind for him. He took her in his arms and said, "I've always wanted a place like this. It will be the first home I've had since I was a boy that I can really call my own. Ma, I think we're going to be very happy here."

But there was one major obstacle. Raoul Walsh wanted fifty thousand dollars for the ranch. Faced with a huge property settlement for his wife, Gable didn't think he could raise the money. Lombard saved the day by putting up the fifty thousand. They closed the deal immediately.

But now that they had the house, another problem presented itself. They could not move in until they were married.

At age ten, Carole Lombard was already a beauty. Two years later, she made her film debut in "A Perfect Crime."

"The King" in 1925, still a lowly "extra" and, from the looks of him, hardly star material.

Lombard and her first husband, William Powell, photographed soon after their wedding in 1931. The marriage lasted 28 months, but they remained close friends.

Lombard and Russ Columbo at a Hollywood nightclub in 1934, just prior to the crooner's allegedly accidental death.

Gable and his second wife, Ria (far right) at a Hollywood preview, 1932. With the Gables are, from left, Douglas Fairbanks, Jr., Mr. and Mrs. Robert Montgomery, Joan Crawford and her father-in-law, Douglas Fairbanks.

Lombard teases Gable by presenting him with a smoked ham with his picture on it during the 1932 filming of "No Man of Her Own," their only movie together.

Claudette Colbert and her hostess strike a playful pose at Lombard's "fun party" at the Venice Amusement Pier in 1935.

Gable and Lombard at the races, one of their first dates after their meeting at "The White Mayfair" Ball, early in 1936.

BOTH PHOTOS: CULVER PICTURES

Lombard with some of her pets, including Pushface, the Pekingese that after its death was stuffed and presented to her as a Christmas gift.

Gable, sporting sideburns for "Parnell," shows off the cougar cub that proved too wild for Lombard's little menagerie.

Gable and Lombard arriving at Jean Harlow's funeral at Forest Lawn Memorial Park, June 1937.

Below left: In a reversal of roles, columnist Walter Winchell woos Lombard while Gable takes notes at William Randolph Hearst's costume birthday ball in 1937.

Below right: Lombard and Fredric March admire her straitjacketing of director William Wellman at the conclusion of the filming of "Nothing Sacred," 1937.

UNITED PRESS INTERNATIONAL   CULVER PICTURES

Gable and Lombard at their grandest, attending the Hollywood premiere of "Marie Antoinette," 1938.

Mr. and Mrs. Clark Gable. The first picture of the newlyweds following their elopement in March 1939.

Despite his displeasure with the deal, Gable forces a grin as Louis B. Mayer signs him over to David O. Selznick for "Gone With the Wind."

Below left: Gable and Lombard in the motorcade leading to the Atlanta world premiere of "Gone With the Wind," December 1939.

Below right: The Gables pose with Marion Davies and director Raoul Walsh at the Hollywood premiere of "Gone With the Wind."

UNITED PRESS INTERNATIONAL   CULVER PICTURES

Gable and Lombard on the lawn of their home, which became known as "The House of the Two Gables."

Below left: One of the Gables' favorite photographs of themselves at home.

Below right: Gable and Lombard sitting on the tailgate of their specially equipped Dodge station wagon, which they used on hunting trips.

Gable testing a new life raft before setting off on another hunting and fishing expedition with Lombard.

"The happy, carefree couple are seen taking life easy and enjoying the rich California sunshine as they rest from their strenuous work," said the caption for this publicity photo.

BOTH PHOTOS: CULVER PICTURES

Gable and Lombard arriving at Johns Hopkins Medical Center in Baltimore, December 1940. He was treated for a shoulder injury while she underwent gynecological tests.

Gable and Lombard celebrating their first wedding anniversary in the MGM commissary. Gable's co-workers surprised them with the cake.

The Gables feeding their chickens. Attempts at marketing "The King's Eggs" were unsuccessful.

The last photograph of Carole Lombard, with her mother, Mrs. Elizabeth Peters, taken in their Indianapolis hotel suite at the conclusion of the bond tour.

BOTH PHOTOS: UNITED PRESS INTERNATIONAL

Carole Lombard's final public appearance, on the stage of Cadle Tabernacle in Indianapolis, January 1942.

The rescue party prepares to remove the bodies from the wreckage of Carole Lombard's plane.

With their eyes closed against the splashing champagne, Gable, Fieldsie Lang, Irene Dunne and Louis B. Mayer attend the launching of the Liberty Ship *Carole Lombard*, January 1944.

Lady Sylvia Ashley, Gable's fourth wife, decided she couldn't live in Carole Lombard's shadow. The marriage lasted only 16 months.

Gable's fifth wife, Kay Williams, patterned herself after Lombard in many ways. Their only child, John Clark, was born after Gable's death.

nine

An Easy Elopement

Marriage plans finally started taking shape in December 1938, when Gable and Lombard found themselves involved in what promised to become one of Hollywood's biggest scandals. *Photoplay*, the most influential and widely read movie magazine of that time, came out with an article entitled "Hollywood's Unmarried Husbands and Wives," which dealt with the unconventional living arrangements of Gable and Lombard, Robert Taylor and Barbara Stanwyck, Charles Chaplin and Paulette Goddard, Constance Bennett and Gilbert Roland, and George Raft and Virginia Pine.

"Unwed couples they might be termed," the article said. "But they go everywhere together; do everything in pairs. No hostess would think of inviting them separately or pairing them with another. They solve one another's problems, handle each other's business affairs. They build houses near each other, buy land in bunches, take up each other's hobbies, father or mother each other's children —even correct each other's clothes—each other's personalities. Yet to the world, their official status is 'just friends.' No more."

When it got around to Gable and Lombard, the article noted that "For Clark, Carole stopped, almost overnight, being a Hollywood playgirl. People are expected to change when they get married. The necessary adaptation to a new life and another personality shows up in every bride and groom. All Clark and Carole did was strike up a Hollywood twosome. Nobody said 'I do!' . . . Yes, Carole Lombard is a changed woman since she tied up with Clark Gable. But her name is still Carole Lombard. The altar record, in fact, among Hollywood's popular twosomes is surprisingly slim. Usually something formidable stands in the way of a marriage certificate when Hollywood stars pair up minus a preacher. In Clark and Carole's case, of course, there is a very sound legal barrier. Clark's still officially a married man. Every now and then negotiations for a divorce are started, but, until something happens in court, Ria Gable is still the only wife the law of the land allows Clark Gable."

Although its points were made almost entirely through innuendo, "Hollywood's Unmarried Husbands and Wives" was considered the most outspoken article about the private lives of the stars ever published up until that time. The piece was apparently written to test the stiff restrictions placed on the fan magazines by the movie industry's self-governing censorship organization. If that was its purpose, the article failed. *Photoplay* was forced to run a public apology the next month, and the studios clamped down more stringently than ever on the fan magazines.

That January 1939 issue of *Photoplay* sold out within hours after it hit the newsstands in the second week of December 1938. Newspapers quoted bits and pieces of "Hollywood's Unmarried Husbands and Wives" out of context, blowing it up into a national sensation. Will Hays, the movies' censorship "Czar," was bombarded with complaints from members of outraged groups like the National Catholic Legion of Decency, the Daughters of the American Revolution, the General Federation of Women's Clubs, the American Legion and the Knights of Columbus, all sounding similar demands that could be summed up in four words: "Get those bums married!"

Since Clark Gable and Robert Taylor were the only two stars

among the "unmarried husbands and wives" who were tied to one studio, MGM, they were to bear the brunt of Will Hays's complaint to Louis B. Mayer. The studio head was very protective of MGM's dignified, ultrarespectable image, having managed over the years to keep it relatively unsoiled, largely through his own personal efforts. In 1932, Mayer had dismissed William Haines, one of the studio's leading stars, for alleged homonsexual misconduct. Three other major challenges to MGM's sanctity, the Gable-Joan Crawford affair and the mysterious deaths of Jean Harlow and husband Paul Bern, were also effectively hushed up by Mayer.

Mayer was especially concerned over Gable's involvement in this new scandal because of its possible negative effect on "Gone With the Wind," in which MGM was investing more than a million dollars. Mayer told Gable that he must settle his problems with his wife and start divorce proceedings as soon as possible. Mayer said that while he could not, of course, force Gable into marrying Carole Lombard, he hoped that would happen.

Mayer, who'd been siding with Ria Gable and encouraging her to make prohibitive demands on her husband, got caught in a trap of his own making. Gable told Mayer that he couldn't pay his wife's demands, which were now in the area of $300,000, without financial help from MGM. Though Gable's contract was not due to expire for two years, Mayer agreed to pay him an advance against the new one, in which his salary was to be increased from $5,000 to $7,500 per week.

December 14, 1938, was one of the happiest days of Carole Lombard's life—Gable finally made a public announcement that he was ready to seek a divorce from his wife. Lombard's joy was short-lived, however, for within twenty-four hours, Mrs. Gable denied that she was getting a divorce, claiming she'd known nothing of Gable's intentions until reading about them in the newspapers. Since she considered herself the wronged party in the affair, she was miffed over Gable's taking the initiative, and she thought she should be the one seeking the divorce. Matters were to drag on for several more months before they reached their resolution.

In the meantime, Carole Lombard was so broken up when her favorite Pekingese, Pushface, died of old age that she couldn't bear to dispose of her pet. She asked the maid to get rid of the corpse for her.

It was the holiday season and Lombard had invited Gable for Christmas dinner at her house. The festivities started in rather macabre fashion when Lombard discovered that one of her gifts was a stuffed Pushface. Instead of disposing of the dead dog, the maid had taken it to a taxidermist as a Christmas surprise. The sight of the glassy-eyed, inanimate Peke made Lombard violently ill. She cried and screamed until it was taken away.

Lombard gave Gable a ruby ring and a Brownie box camera that Christmas. Gable promptly turned the camera back to Lombard, and she always used it to keep a record of their life together. Gable had two gifts for Lombard, both of which were too large to bring into the house. Waiting for her outside the front door was a two-hundred-pound lifesized plaster statue of Gable, which had been sent to him at MGM by a secret admirer in Wichita, Kansas. Lombard said she'd use the statue as a hatrack until they moved to the ranch, where she would turn it into a hitching post for their horses. Gable's second gift to Lombard was parked in the driveway—a yellow Cadillac convertible. It was the most generous gift Gable had ever made to anyone.

But the gift that Carole Lombard wanted most that year was delivered elsewhere—at David Selznick's home in Beverly Hills, where the producer was holding a small Christmas party for friends and business associates. Vivien Leigh, a young British actress who'd come to Hollywood to visit her lover, Laurence Olivier, had been told that her screen tests were a success, that the part of Scarlett O'Hara was hers.

Carole Lombard was heartbroken when she heard that Vivien Leigh had the role, and Lombard's agent, Myron Selznick, who also represented Leigh, had a lot of explaining to do before she calmed down. He tried to soften the blow by negotiating an advantageous deal for Lombard at RKO for two pictures annually for two years.

Her new contract made her one of the first stars in Hollywood to receive a percentage of the profits of her pictures, which was to be paid in addition to her $150,000 salary.

Lombard's first picture for RKO was to be a melodrama, "In Name Only," with Cary Grant as her leading man. She could easily identify with the character she was playing, a woman in love with an unhappily married man whose mercenary wife refuses to give him a divorce. Lombard warned Gable that if his own divorce hadn't taken place by the time "In Name Only" started, she was going to offer Ria Gable the part of the other woman.

As if Gable didn't have enough to worry about with his domestic problems, he was unhappy with the way "Gone With the Wind" was progressing. His costumes fit badly, the script was constantly being rewritten, David Selznick was insisting that he attempt a Southern accent. Very early in the morning of the day he was to report to work, Gable was awakened out of a deep sleep by a messenger boy. By motorcycle, Selznick had sent Gable a ninety-two-page memo outlining exactly how he wanted his star to play Rhett Butler.

Gable arrived at his dressing room that first day to find that Lombard had anticipated his belligerent mood by draping the mirror with a string of stuffed doves, stressing the need for peace and understanding. On the dresser was a beautifully wrapped package which Lombard had also sent to brighten Gable's day. Inside was a knitted "cockwarmer" with Lombard's handwritten instructions: "Don't let it get cold. Bring it home hot for me."

Gable's first scene in "Gone With the Wind" called for him to present Vivien Leigh with a fancy Paris hat. This was Gable's first exposure to working with director George Cukor other than in rehearsals. Gable didn't care for the slow, methodical way that Cukor set up the scene. It reminded Gable too much of his experience with John Stahl on "Parnell," the most agonizing and trying of his career.

Gable also thought that George Cukor was paying too much attention to Vivien Leigh and he felt excluded from the close personal relationship that had developed between them. Gable doubted that he could establish the same kind of rapport with Cukor, who was a fussy, gossipy man of great sensitivity and sophistication, too complex a person for Gable to have much in common with. Gable preferred the company of outdoorsy adventuresome men like Victor Fleming and Jack Conway, who were great buddies of his, as well as his usual directors at MGM. They were also expert at handling Gable, knew his limitations as an actor and emphasized the natural, likable and two-fisted persona he had acquired over the years.

Gable resented the way George Cukor kept at him about his Southern accent, finally complaining to David Selznick. The producer, who didn't want to antagonize his star after waiting so long and sacrificing so much to get him, took Gable's side and reprimanded Cukor. But the run-in intensified Selznick's fears that he might have to find a new director. Cukor was running five days behind schedule, and both Selznick and L. B. Mayer were dissatisfied with some of the scenes he'd shot. They felt that Cukor was placing too much emphasis on character and intimate detail, failing to give the scenes the size and scope that the public would expect in a multimillion-dollar spectacle of this type.

Two and a half weeks after he'd started directing "Gone With the Wind," George Cukor was dismissed. With the picture now certain to exceed its $2,000,000 budget because of this delay, MGM insisted that Selznick use one of its own contract directors. Since Gable had been so unhappy with Cukor, Selznick gave him a voice in the matter. Gable selected Victor Fleming, who was then in the final stages of directing "The Wizard of Oz."

But Selznick had a rude awakening when Victor Fleming told him, "David, your fucking script is no fucking good." Selznick panicked, shutting down production for two weeks while he consulted his favorite script doctor, Ben Hecht. Selznick paid Hecht $15,000 to rewrite the script, against a seven-day deadline. In the end, Selznick was still not satisfied with the script. It was to be constantly rewritten throughout the balance of production, often by Selznick himself.

While Gable was on this enforced vacation from "Gone With the Wind," his lawyers and Ria's finally reached a tentative agreement on a property settlement. Gable was to pay his wife $286,000, plus any income taxes involved. This meant that he would have settled over half a million dollars on Ria Gable since their separation in 1935.

To further soothe Mrs. Gable's feelings, her lawyers insisted that Gable should issue the following statement to the press: "I regret bitterly that a short time ago a story was printed to the effect that I would seek a divorce from Mrs. Gable. Mrs. Gable and I had a fine life together until the time came that we both realized we could no longer make a go of it. After years of separation, it is only natural that Mrs. Gable should institute proceedings that will assure her freedom."

But Ria Gable still had to have the last, bitchy word. When she arrived in Las Vegas to start the proceedings, she told reporters, "Clark knew he could have a divorce any time, but he never seemed to want one. I think a marriage between a movie star and a society woman has a better chance of succeeding than one between two stars."

The divorce was granted in a four-minute hearing on March 8, 1939. Ria Gable spent the day in bed, weeping and wailing, with a masseuse, hairdresser and manicurist trying to console her. MGM dispatched one of its publicists to stay with her in case she tried to say something uncomplimentary about Gable and Lombard to the newspapers.

Lombard was at RKO posing for publicity stills when the news of the divorce broke. Up until then, she had never made a public statement about her feelings for Gable or about their plans to marry. But now, when Louella Parsons called her, Lombard had no hesitation about telling her that the wedding would take place soon, though they had no definite plans as yet. "When Clark gets a few days off, perhaps we'll sneak away and have the ceremony performed," Lombard said.

Her hint of an elopement set reporters to establishing a day-

and-night watch on Lombard's house in Bel-Air. In the next few days the couple received piles of telegrams and letters from hotels, airlines, chambers of commerce and justices of the peace suggesting a time and place for their wedding. Lombard told Gable she was afraid their wedding was going to develop into a "fucking circus," that they would have to find a way of sneaking off quietly somewhere without anyone knowing about it.

Otto Winkler, the press agent who handled most of Gable's personal publicity at MGM, was sent out on a reconaissance mission to find some remote spot for the marriage. The place finally settled on was Kingman, Arizona, a small town of only a couple of thousand people, located about 400 miles from Los Angeles.

On March 28, Gable discovered that he would have the next two days off, due to sudden changes in the shooting schedule of "Gone With the Wind." When he phoned Lombard to tell her that they could use that time for the wedding, she was so overjoyed that she let out an Indian war whoop she hadn't used since her early days in Buck Jones Westerns.

Although they were concerned that news of their elopement would leak to the press, the lovers had a lucky break. 20th Century-Fox had taken the whole Hollywood press corps on a junket to San Francisco for the world premiere of "The Story of Alexander Graham Bell" and they would not be back until the following day.

Otto Winkler and his boss, Howard Strickling, persuaded Gable and Lombard to hold a press conference at her house the morning after the wedding. Since the round-trip drive to Kingman was about 800 miles, the couple would have to rush through the wedding ceremony and return immediately. There was no chance of their spending their wedding night alone together, not that it really mattered much at this stage of their more than three-year affair.

The Gable-Lombard elopement was one of the most unglamorous on record. Packing their wedding clothes in a suitcase, they made the trip in their shabbiest shirts and dungarees, with Lombard wearing no make-up and her hair tied in pigtails. They traveled in Otto Winkler's blue DeSoto coupe, which had a rumble seat in the back. Before they left, Winkler's wife loaded them up with sandwiches and thermoses of coffee and water to sustain them on their long journey. Gable took turns driving with Otto Winkler, who was to act as his best man. Whenever they had to stop for gas, they'd first pull up to the side of the road and Gable would hide in the rumble seat in order not to be recognized.

Just before they crossed into Arizona, Lombard insisted they stop to buy some flowers for the wedding. Gable grudgingly peeled a dollar bill from the big wad in his pocket and told Winkler he expected some change. Winkler bought a corsage of lilies of the valley and pink roses for Lombard and carnation boutonnieres for Gable and himself. Gable was pleased when Winkler gave him 50 cents back.

As they drove along, Gable kept mumbling, "I still can't believe the day has come." Lombard gripped Gable's arm tightly, feeling so happy that she was silent for one of the few times in her life.

They reached Kingman around four in the afternoon, driving straight to the town hall. The clerk on duty in the marriage bureau recognized Gable immediately and became so confused she couldn't speak. Fumbling for the necessary forms, she splattered ink on them as she handed Gable a pen to fill them out. Gable gave his age as thirty-eight and his occupation as "an actor." Lombard fibbed about her age by a year when she stated she was twenty-nine.

Otto Winkler had made arrangements with the minister of the First Methodist-Episcopal Church to perform the ceremony, although he had not revealed the identity of the friends he was representing. When Gable and Lombard arrived at the rectory, the minister and his wife were very cordial, but did not seem unduly impressed by the famous couple. The lovers were taken to separate rooms to change into their wedding clothes. Gable put on a blue serge suit, white shirt and printed tie. Since Lombard had been married once before, she felt she couldn't wear white, but she had selected a light-gray flannel suit, padded at the shoulders and delicately tapered at the waist. With it she wore a gray-and-white polka-dotted vest and gray accessories. The entire ensemble was created for her by the noted designer Irene, who was now designing most of her film and street clothes.

If the wedding ceremony had been performed in Hollywood, it surely would have been another MGM spectacular, due to the importance of the principals involved. In Kingman it was conducted in a quiet dignified way. Lombard cried. Gable was so confused that, before he was even asked for it, he gave the minister the platinum band he had been carrying around in his pocket for three months.

After the ceremony, Lombard phoned her mother to tell her the news. Gable got on the line, sounding more like a delighted teen-ager than the great lover of the movies when he said, "This is your new son-in-law, Mom." There was no time for a big romantic scene. The newlyweds immediately started back for Los Angeles, holding hands while Otto Winkler drove.

On the outskirts of Kingman, Winkler stopped to telegraph details of the wedding to the MGM publicity department. Lombard was concerned about her friend, Louella Parsons, receiving just a standard press handout and she insisted on sending Parsons and her boss, William Randolph Hearst, separate telegrams which simply said, "Married this afternoon. Carole and Clark." Not even the King of Hollywood and his new queen could afford to offend the waspish columnist and her publisher.

Soon after the wedding party crossed back into California, they stopped at a Harvey House restaurant. The flabbergasted manager and waitresses offered to clear out the whole dining room when they recognized Gable and Lombard, who insisted on sitting at the counter, where Gable ordered the biggest steaks in the house for their wedding dinner. While they were waiting to be served, a customer timidly asked them for their autographs. For the first time, Lombard was able to sign hers "Carole Gable."

Gable and Lombard returned to her house in Bel-Air at three in the morning, almost twenty-four hours from the time they had left. Lombard's family was there to greet them, but the newlyweds were so tired that they went to Lombard's bedroom to try to get some rest before the press conference. Lombard gave a shriek of laughter when she discovered that her brothers had hung a shotgun over the bed.

MGM assigned two of its uniformed policemen to stand guard outside Lombard's house to keep curiosity-seekers away from the press conference later that morning. Gable and Lombard made their grand entrance down the staircase in her living room, smiling proudly and nervously clutching each other's arms as they posed for pictures in their wedding clothes.

The reporters started firing questions at the Gables. Gable said they wouldn't be able to take a honeymoon because of their picture commitments, but that they were hoping to make up for it by visiting the New York World's Fair when it opened. Lombard admitted she could cook: "Damn well, too, but I don't know what Pappy's favorite dishes are yet." One reporter wanted to know if the Gables were planning to have children. Lombard giggled and Gable looked embarrassed. The reporter plowed on and asked if they thought that careers and marriage could mix. Gable said, "We'd rather not answer that."

Another reporter expressed surprise at the subdued, unspectacular nature of the Gables' wedding. He said that Hollywood felt a bit cheated that Lombard hadn't pulled an outrageous gag or come out with some kind of explosive statement. Lombard smiled and shrugged her questioner off. There were no words she could think of that could express how seriously she took her marriage vows, which were the last thing in the world she could ever joke about.

Louella Parsons was too important a personage to come to the press conference. When Lombard called her afterward to apologize for not giving her an exclusive on the wedding story, Parsons sounded somewhat put out, but said she understood. She asked Lombard about her plans for the future. Lombard said, "I'll work for a few more years and then I want a family. I'll let Pa be the star and I'll stay home, darn the socks and look after the kids." Lombard was often in a frivolous mood with Parsons, knowing that the columnist literally wet her pants when she laughed. But this time, Lombard wasn't joshing.

ten

The House of Two Gables

Clark Gable and Carole Lombard had an advantage over many newlywed couples of that time, in that they had few post-nuptial adjustments to make to each other. Their life together went on pretty much as it had for the past thirty-nine months, the major difference being that their union was now legal.

The sexual side of this relationship, both before and after the wedding, was not so basic or all-consuming as might have been expected of the wantonish Lombard and "What-a-Man" Gable, because Gable was a barely adequate lover. Lombard herself once told a friend, "My God, you know how I love Pa, but I can't say he's a helluva good lay."

Lombard traced Gable's inexpertness to his being "sex-starved for years" and blamed it on his two older wives, claiming that they were easily gratified and never gave him a chance to develop any technique.

Lombard was very tender and giving with Gable in their physical relations, and he did, in time and with his wife's encouragement, improve as a lover—but not to the degree that it could be said that sex was what held the couple together.

Gable moved into Lombard's house in Bel-Air right after

their wedding, since renovations on the ranch wouldn't be completed until the early summer. Lombard said she wanted "The King" to have a castle worthy of him and she was doing most of the decorating herself. She had the rare gift of being able to visualize everything in advance, and had planned the color schemes and ordered the furniture in a day. She wanted it to be Gable's house—very masculine and casually comfortable, a place where he could put his big feet up on a coffee table and not be afraid of breaking some delicate little knickknack.

Most of the furniture, especially anything that Gable was likely to use, was being custom made to king-sized specifications. At Lombard's insistence, the sofas, chairs and Gable's bed were all to be at least a third larger than average. Even the drinking glasses that she bought on one of her frequent shopping sprees were gigantic, the size of old-fashioned preserve jars.

Gable and Lombard were both eager to finish their current pictures, "Gone With the Wind" and "In Name Only," so that they could devote themselves fully to their new home. Lombard found that Gable wasn't grumbling so much, now that his friend, Victor Fleming, had taken over direction of "Gone With the Wind."

But there were times when even Fleming could not help Gable, who was very self-conscious about his rugged public image. He had a terrible time preparing himself for his most difficult scene in "Gone With the Wind," in which he had to break down and cry when he heard that Scarlett O'Hara had miscarried after a fall that he had provoked.

Gable was afraid that his tears would stir the opposite reaction of laughter from the audience. Victor Fleming tried to reason with him that crying would only heighten the audience's sympathy for him, but Gable was dubious.

The night before the scene was filmed, Gable couldn't sleep and complained of stomach cramps. Lombard sat up with him most of the night, hoping that any encouragement from her might help him overcome his reticence and embarrassment about crying. At the studio the next day, Olivia de Havilland, who was appearing in the scene with Gable, also tried to calm his fears.

But Gable, still uneasy, fussed and fumed in his dressing room, complaining that he was sorry he'd ever taken up acting. Threatening to chuck it all and become a farmer, he asked Victor Fleming if they couldn't rewrite the scene or eliminate it entirely. They compromised by shooting the scene twice. First they did it Gable's way, with his back to the camera so that he wouldn't have to show his grief. Then they filmed the scene over again, catching Gable with his face full of remorse, his eyes wet with tears.

The crew applauded when Gable finished the second take, but he still wasn't convinced that it should be used in the picture. Fleming took him to a screening of the rushes to reassure him. When Gable saw himself crying, he was so pleasantly surprised by his convincing performance that he turned to Fleming and said, "I don't believe it. What the hell happened?" Later, when Carole Lombard saw it, she said it was the best bit of acting Gable had ever done.

"Gone With the Wind" was fraught with more problems than any picture Gable had ever worked on. Throughout most of the filming, he was caught uncomfortably in the middle of a raging battle between Victor Fleming and Vivien Leigh. Gable had grown fond of Leigh. Possessed of a real Irish temper, she could curse with the best of them, though no match for Carole Lombard. Gable felt great sympathy for Leigh, who, in her love affair with Laurence Olivier, was experiencing many of the problems Gable had with Lombard. Leigh had a husband and a child back in London, and Olivier was also married. David Selznick and Louis B. Mayer were doing everything possible to keep the romance looking respectable, out of fear of another "Unmarried Husbands and Wives" blow-up.

Because of his fondness for Leigh and his friendship with Fleming, Gable tried not to take sides in their constant squabbles. Leigh was uncertain of Gable's loyalties and never confided in him about her problems. But Fleming was after Gable all the time, looking for sympathy. Gable would take him to his dressing room and pour him a few drinks. Fleming, also operating under great pressure from David Selznick, was growing very morose. One morning, he told Gable he had almost driven off a cliff on his way to work.

Finally Fleming's nerves got the best of him. During a rehearsal, he blew up when Vivien Leigh kept resisting his instructions to put more bitchiness into the reading of her lines. "I can't be a bitch," Leigh said. Fleming glared at her for a moment, then, shouting, "Miss Leigh, you can stick this script up your royal British ass," he threw the script on the floor and headed straight home to bed, complaining that he was too ill to return to work.

David Selznick couldn't afford to shut down production while Fleming recuperated, so he hired another director, Sam Wood, to take over temporarily. When Victor Fleming returned two weeks later, Selznick retained Sam Wood and kept both directors working on different scenes to make up for lost time.

When Gable said it would be too confusing for him to work under two directors, Selznick had to promise him that all his scenes would be directed by Fleming. Vivien Leigh, Olivia de Havilland and Leslie Howard weren't so lucky, often being directed by Fleming for half the day and by Wood for the other half, which made it very difficult to maintain a consistent performance.

Lombard completed "In Name Only" early in June 1939, and was ready for the move to the ranch by the time Gable finished work in "Gone With the Wind" two weeks later. On Gable's last day, David Selznick presented him with an antique pine desk, one of the props from the picture, as a housewarming gift.

Their new white brick-and-frame home had a gabled roof and was soon being referred to by Hollywood punsters as "The House of the Two Gables." Lombard had decorated it in Early American style, and by movie-star standards, it was quite unspectacular. There was no private projection room, no tennis court, not even a swimming pool. When asked why, Lombard once said, "If we put in everything at once, we'll have nothing to look forward to."

The focal point of the house was Gable's gun room on the main floor. One wall was covered by a glass case containing fifty antique pistols and rifles, and this collection was constantly expanding as Gable's friends and fans made new additions. The living room was done very simply using a yellow-and-green color scheme. The dining room was patterned after an Early American tavern, with a long, narrow table and a chandelier of antique oil lamps, wired for electricity.

Upstairs, where Gable and Lombard each had their own bedroom suites, a more traditional Hollywood note was discernible. The walls and ceilings of Lombard's dressing room and bath were completely mirrored, thick white rugs covered the floors, and the fixtures were of white marble, silver and crystal. Lombard liked to call it "the most elegant shithouse in the San Fernando Valley."

Gable's suite was also grandiose. Hidden in the wall near his bed was a fully stocked bar, which Lombard had had specially built. She had no intentions of going all the way downstairs to fix him his usual nightcap.

Gable and Lombard found a plumber still at work in the kitchen the day they were moving in. When he told them that the work might not be finished that day, Lombard reacted by letting loose with a barrage of her favorite curse words. While Gable was generally amused by her profanity, he disapproved of her using it to lash out at anyone. Dragging Lombard by the hand into the next room and jerking her violently into his arms, he said, "Listen, baby, if there's any cussing to be done, I'm man enough to do it myself."

Stunned, Lombard glared rebelliously at him, then suddenly softened and dropped her head on his chest. Throwing her arms around him and bursting into tears she said, "I've waited a long time for somebody to do that. Oh, Pa, I'm glad I love you. I'm so glad I married you."

They spent most of that first summer at the ranch settling in and relaxing. Gable had a sorrel show horse named Sunny, while Lombard's bay polo pony was called Melody. The Gables generally went riding in the late afternoon, then raced home to watch the sunset from their patio, Gable sipping Scotch and Lombard her favorite Coca-Cola.

Though they hoped to put the ranch on a self-sustaining

basis, their initial effort was discouraging. Gable bought a cow, but when it didn't give much milk, he sent it back. Lombard quipped that it must have been the most humiliated cow in the world, having been rejected by Clark Gable. A new cow was an improvement. But by the time Gable bought processing equipment, Lombard figured that their milk was costing them between four and five dollars a quart.

Two crises that summer left the Gables shaken. One morning, while Gable was alone in the house, a teen-ager broke in and stole one of his guns. Gable accidentally stumbled upon the intruder before he could make his escape, and easily overpowered him. In the struggle, the loaded gun went flying but luckily did not go off. Lombard was very upset when Gable told her of the incident. It reminded her all too vividly of Russ Columbo's accidental shooting.

Lombard was preparing to play a nurse in "Vigil in the Night." Gable, knowing how she lived her parts off screen, wondered how long it would be before she pounced on him to check his pulse or administer an enema. But ironically, Lombard ended up the patient. Late one night, she started complaining of severe abdominal pains, which turned out to be acute appendicitis. She was operated on several hours later, after Gable rushed her to Cedars of Lebanon Hospital.

Gable arranged to stay in the room next to Lombard's, sleeping there for the duration of her hospitalization. On her last night, Gable arrived later than usual and found most of the lights out. Guessing that Lombard might be asleep, he tiptoed into her darkened room to kiss her goodnight. All of a sudden, a pair of unfamiliar arms embraced him and he received a big, sloppy kiss from lips that he was sure weren't his wife's. When he struggled to his feet and switched on the light, he discovered a fat, middle-aged woman in Lombard's bed, with a smile of pure ecstasy on her face. Gable finally found Lombard in a room a few doors away. She swore to him, with her fingers crossed behind her back, that she'd had nothing to do with changing the rooms.

Although Lombard recovered quickly from the operation, she

apparently took her appendectomy as another omen of impending danger to herself. On August 8, 1939, just days after the operation, she drew up a new will, naming Gable as the sole executor and major beneficiary of her estate. Concerned about her mother's future welfare, she willed Bessie Peters an annuity. Lombard also left a smaller annuity to her best friend, Fieldsie, who was now married to director Walter Lang.

Lombard was about four weeks into "Vigil in the Night" when Gable started working in "Strange Cargo" at MGM. Lombard liked the idea of their both working simultaneously, since it meant their layoffs would also occur at the same time. She told Gable that in the future she would always try to arrange her working schedule to coincide with his, so that they would have as much free time together as possible. As a free lance, she had more flexibility than Gable had under his contract at MGM. During their marriage, Lombard was to turn down a fortune in film assignments because her husband and their life together were more important to her.

"Strange Cargo" teamed Gable with Joan Crawford for the first time in three years. Gable felt uncomfortable about working with Crawford again, and his new wife didn't make things any easier. While Lombard didn't consider the actress as a threat to their marriage, she loved to tease Gable by threatening to come down to the set with a loaded shotgun if she heard any rumors. Adding to Gable's disquiet was the fact that Crawford was a single woman again, having divorced her second husband, Franchot Tone.

While filming "Strange Cargo," Gable was approached about attending the world premiere of "Gone With the Wind" in Atlanta, Georgia, the home of author Margaret Mitchell. For months, David Selznick and MGM had been planning a three-day series of events. There were to be all sorts of parades, parties and dances to celebrate the launching of the $3,700,000 epic, and the governor of Georgia had declared a state holiday.

But Gable, who still hadn't gotten over his feeling that he'd been shanghaied into making "Gone With the Wind" by Mayer and Selznick, refused to participate. He was also very self-conscious and shy in big crowds. He thought he'd look ridiculous as a conquering hero at the kind of ticker-tape-and-confetti reception planned for the stars when they arrived in Atlanta.

Lombard told Gable he would be making a big mistake if he didn't attend the premiere. She felt that Rhett Butler was the greatest part Gable had ever played, the one that the public would most remember him for.

Gable finally said he would go if Lombard went with him. She hesitated, mindful that her presence might detract attention from Gable and spoil his moment of triumph. But when he persisted, she agreed to accompany him. MGM didn't want Lombard along, since she had had nothing to do with "Gone With the Wind." Then Gable found out that Vivien Leigh was being accompanied by Laurence Olivier. When Gable insisted that if Leigh's lover could go along, then he should be permitted to take his wife, the studio reluctantly agreed.

MGM chartered a DC-3 passenger plane from American Airlines to fly the Gables to Atlanta. Otto Winkler, who'd been the best man at their wedding, was accompanying his friends. Winkler had never flown before and was very nervous. Lombard sat with him, holding his hand until he calmed down. Teasingly she said, "If we're going to crash, we might as well go together." Nobody took the prophetic comment very seriously then.

The Gables' plane landed in Atlanta just a few minutes after another one carrying David Selznick, Vivien Leigh, Laurence Olivier and Olivia de Havilland. Leslie Howard, the fourth star of "Gone With the Wind," was not attending the premiere. He had returned to England to participate in his country's war effort against Germany.

There was another war being celebrated in Atlanta, and from the looks of it the South had won it. Thousands of people lined the streets, dressed in Civil War and antebellum costumes. Aged veterans of the war were out parading in their Confederate uniforms, while street musicians played "Dixie" on most every corner. Three hundred thousand people, more than had participated in the original Battle of Atlanta, crowded the route of the seven-mile motor-cade that conducted the stars from the airport to their hotel.

Gable and Lombard sat in the back of an open Packard convertible, waving to the spectators. A woman in an old-fashioned gown peeled off one of her long lace gloves and hurled it at Gable. Lombard told him to beware, that a pair of bloomers would probably be the next tribute.

That night, Gable and Lombard attended a dress ball, staged on the actual charity bazaar set from "Gone With the Wind," which had been shipped in sections from Hollywood at a cost of $10,000. Gable, Vivien Leigh and Olivia de Havilland made their grand entrances at the ball dressed in their film costumes while Lombard, wearing a black velvet evening dress and carrying a silver fox muff, watched from a box seat. She was besieged by autograph hunters but insisted on signing simply "Carole Gable." A fan told her that the value of her autograph had increased by fourteen cents since her marriage.

The premiere showing of "Gone With the Wind" was held at Loew's Grand Theatre, the façade of which had been transformed into a replica of Twelve Oaks, one of the stately mansions in the film. When the Gables arrived, the enormous crowd of spectators let out the Confederate rebel yell. Gable threw his hands in the air to silence the throng and over the public address system thanked them for their reception.

Out in the theater lobby, Gable and Lombard met Margaret Mitchell for the first time. She was a tiny woman who reached barely to Gable's shoulders. When Lombard asked the author if she'd had Gable in mind when she created Rhett Butler, Mitchell denied it, confessing she'd never even seen a Gable film until she heard he was being considered for the movie and then caught him in "San Francisco" at her neighborhood theater.

The Gables sat with Margaret Mitchell and her husband, John Marsh, during the unreeling of the saga. The capacity audience cheered and applauded throughout the film, especially at every mention of the gallant South and whenever strains of "Dixie" were heard on the sound track. Watching the scene in which Scarlett is nursing wounded soldiers and the camera draws back to reveal thousands of Confederate troops, Margaret Mitchell leaned over to Gable and whispered, "Mah Gawd, if we'd-ah had as many soldiers as that, we'd ah won the woah."

Margaret Mitchell was too shy to acknowledge the applause at the end of the picture, so Carole Lombard finally said to the author, "Come on, honey, I'll help you." She took Mitchell by the hand and led her up on the stage. Mitchell stood there a moment, nervously twisting her handkerchief before she thanked everyone in behalf of "me and my poor Scarlett."

On the third and final day of the premiere celebration, Margaret Mitchell gave a luncheon in honor of the stars at her club. The place was swarming with middle-aged women who had come mainly to see Clark Gable. As he posed for pictures with Mitchell, so many women closed in on him at once that he swept the author up in his arms and carried her off to another room. They remained locked in for fifteen minutes, while the crowd of women subsided.

Gable and Lombard were exhausted by the three days of non-stop events and returned to California in their chartered plane that afternoon. Shortly after they checked out of their hotel, an elderly woman wearing pince-nez approached the reservations desk and asked if she could have the room that Gable had just vacated. The clerk said yes, but that she'd have to wait until the room was cleaned and the bed made up. The woman asked if it was definitely the same room that Gable had slept in. When the clerk assured her that it was, she said, "I'll take it just as it is, and please make sure they don't change the sheets."

Gable felt that he'd been exploited at the Atlanta premiere. He thought that David Selznick and MGM had capitalized on his name to sell tickets, and he resented that he was never going to see a penny of the film's profits. When the Hollywood premiere came up, he again went into one of his tantrums, refusing to attend, but Lombard, as usual, talked Gable out of it, by threatening to go with his stand-in, Lew Smith.

No amount of Lombard's persuading, however, could convince Gable to go to the party that David Selznick was holding at the Trocadero right after the screening. Gable timed his arrival at the theater at precisely one minute before curtain time. He and Lombard posed briefly for photographers and hurried into the theater. During the intermission, Gable insisted on taking his wife home. He felt that he'd fulfilled his obligations to MGM by attending, that his presence was no longer needed. Lombard, who had bought a new gold lamé gown for the occasion, was hoping that Gable would have a last-minute change of heart and that they'd go on to the party after all. She said that Selznick would be offended if they didn't turn up, but Gable couldn't be swayed that night. They went straight home from the theater.

Gable had nothing to lose by snubbing Selznick, but Lombard did, since she still had a contract with the producer for another picture. That picture was never made. Selznick doubted whether he and Lombard could work harmoniously together again, with Gable hovering suspiciously in the background.

In a confidential memo, Selznick told Lombard: "Neither of us is used to such strained and peculiar situations as that on the night of the local opening of 'Gone with the Wind,' when I like to believe we should have been in each other's arms. I certainly recognize the awkward position you are in, and cannot expect to come out on the right side when your loyalties are divided. And perhaps some day in the future, attitudes may change, as they do in the business, and it will again be possible for you to do a picture for me with the wholehearted pleasure that we once both knew in our endeavors."

eleven

Planning for a Future

For the Gables' first Christmas at the ranch, Lombard bought the biggest evergreen tree she could find, had it sprayed white and decorated it herself with red lights and silver ornaments. Gable's main gift to her that December 1939 was the ruby heart that she always would wear around her neck on a solid gold chain. Lombard gave Gable white silk pajamas and a matching robe, which were custom made to her own design from the last silk to leave China before the Japanese invasion.

The war that was raging in the Far East and in Europe frightened Lombard, who was sure that her own country would eventually be drawn into it. That previous October, when the news came over the radio that England had declared war against Germany, she had broken down in tears and told Gable that she felt that something terrible was going to happen to them. Her greatest fear was that if the United States did enter the war, Gable would be called away from her and their dreams of having a family would never be realized.

Lombard was longing to have a baby. Conscious of the handsome, luminous couple that she and Gable made, she was certain that any children born of their union would have to be extraordinary. Her only New Year's resolution for 1940 was to become pregnant.

Her failure to conceive thus far was already a matter of great concern to Lombard. Always plagued by menstrual problems, she'd been advised by her doctors that childbearing would be difficult, though not impossible.

Hoping that a break from their tense routine of recent months might heighten her chances of conceiving, Gable and Lombard set off on their long-postponed honeymoon trip as soon as he finished "Strange Cargo." Their destination was a hunting club in Baja California, about seventy miles below the U.S.-Mexican border. Gable had recently bought a specially equipped Dodge station wagon with four-wheel drive and a sixty-five-gallon gasoline tank and they loaded up with a tent, groceries, cooking utensils, guns, fishing rods and whatever other equipment they would need. Lombard bought herself a new sleeping bag, which she had fully lined with one of her old mink coats.

Before the Gables left home, Otto Winkler asked if he could join them in Baja later in the week to take some informal publicity pictures. Lombard didn't like such intrusions on their privacy, but Gable was so fond of Winkler that he agreed, saying he would telephone his friend to make arrangements as soon as they arrived at their destination.

The hunting club was situated in a remote mountainous area. When the Gables reached it, they were so tired from being bounced about all day on rutty, unpaved roads that they forgot to phone Otto Winkler. The next day the duck hunting was poor, so they decided to move farther south, where there were brant geese. They put up at a lodge run by two elderly sisters, who knew Gable from previous trips there. It was a primitive setup with a few shacks and a dingy dining room where greasy, generally indigestible food was served. Lombard came down with severe diarrhea and spent most of her time running back and forth to the privy.

Gable's thirty-ninth birthday was coming up the next day and

Lombard persuaded him to drive to Ensenada to celebrate. They left that morning, after the lodge owners presented Gable with a homemade birthday cake. Lombard decorated it with the big white candle that was the only source of light in their one-room shack.

Enroute to Ensenada, the Gables were caught in a thunderstorm. When their station wagon skidded off the slippery mountain road and got stuck in mud, they had to spend the night in the back of the wagon in their sleeping bags. Their groceries depleted by this time, there was only Gable's birthday cake to sustain them. Fortunately, an old Mexican came along carrying a sackful of boiled lobsters, which he was taking to the village market. Apparently he liked the strangers' faces, for he gave Gable and Lombard two lobsters, which enabled them to have a birthday party after all. The lobsters were stringy and overcooked, the cake like plaster, but the hungry Gables devoured everything.

Meanwhile, they were unaware that they were making headlines again. Newspapers all over the country were carrying stories like "Gable Missing With Carole in Mexico" and "Suspect Gable and Bride Kidnapped by Mexican Bandits." When Otto Winkler hadn't heard from his friends, he chartered a plane to fly him to Ensenada. Finding no trace of Gable and Lombard there, he had cabled MGM for help. His telegram somehow got into the hands of the newspaper wire services.

The next morning, the Gables and their station wagon were pulled out of the mud by a passing truck. When they finally reached Ensenada, they found Otto Winkler organizing a search party. Winkler was terribly embarrassed by the incident, as was the Mexican government, which charged it was all a publicity stunt. The Mexican ambassador complained to MGM. Afraid that the company's films might be banned from Mexican theaters, Louis B. Mayer looked for a scapegoat and fired Otto Winkler. Gable was furious and got Winkler reinstated. Though it was the right action to take at the time, Gable regretted the gesture later. If Winkler had left MGM's employ, he would not have been assigned to accompany Carole Lombard on her bond tour.

When the Gables returned home, he learned that he had been nominated for an Academy Award for "Gone With the Wind." It was ironic that the role Gable had fought most violently against playing was turning out to be the high point of his entire career. Lombard thought he was certain to win the Oscar for best actor, but she was wrong. He was betrayed by his own studio, MGM, which swayed its powerful block of voters into backing Robert Donat in "Goodbye, Mr. Chips." The Donat film was a box-office disappointment, needing the publicity of an Oscar far more than "Gone With the Wind."

Gable was the only major "Gone With the Wind" nominee who didn't win. The Selznick production received ten Academy Awards, the most ever presented to a single motion picture up until that time. Gable was not disappointed when he was bypassed. He had never quite recovered from the shock of winning an Oscar six years before for "It Happened One Night," and felt that was recognition enough for what he thought were his meager abilities as an actor.

Just being part of "Gone With the Wind" was reward enough for Gable. From the day it was released, it was, with the possible exception of "Birth of a Nation," the most successful motion picture ever made. It became, for all time, the movie that all others were measured against, and it firmly established Gable's right to the title of "The King of Hollywood."

Although he would always resent not having a share in any of the film's enormous profits, Gable was, by 1940, earning a very decent wage for a man who believed his proper place in life was in the grease pit of a garage. He was just starting a new five-year contract with MGM that paid him $300,000 a year—$7,500 a week for 40 weeks. In ten weeks, Gable earned as much as President Roosevelt did in a year. Writer J. P. McEvoy said this was decidedly unfair, "since FDR is a much better actor."

The Gables were now one of the most affluent couples in Hollywood. Lombard's salary was also averaging $300,000 a year, which gave them a combined income of $600,000. In addition, they each made several radio appearances a year at $5,000 a program, which accounted for another $25,000 to 30,000 annually. Though this placed them in the highest tax bracket, it still left them with about $125,000 a year. When Gable groused about so much of their money going to taxes Lombard could always shut him up by reminding him that if he were working as a garage mechanic, he'd be lucky to be making $30 a week.

By Hollywood standards, the Gables lived quite conservatively. Their annual living expenses were estimated at $16,000, for servants, repairs, property taxes, food and transportation. Their ranch was never as grand as it was made out to be in the fan magazines. It was roughly equivalent to the farms that had suddenly become a fashionable hobby for Broadway stage stars back in the East. Aside from their horses, the Gables had a mule, a couple of cows, some chickens and turkeys. Most of the work was done by a hired farmer and his wife, who lived in a small house on the edge of the property.

Gable and Lombard enjoyed the simple, rustic life at the ranch. When the spirit moved him, Gable worked hard around the place, taking care of the fruit trees, tending the animals and cultivating the soil. When he wasn't working in a picture, he'd rise at seven in the morning, hitch the mule to a mowing machine and cut the grass. Some mornings he'd just drive around the grounds in the little yellow tractor Lombard had given him for his birthday. Home was beginning to mean a great deal to Gable, who hadn't known a real one since the age of fifteen.

Lombard did everything she could to make herself part of the life that so enchanted her husband. She took care of the chickens and supervised the flower beds. It was her idea to try to put the ranch on a paying basis by selling eggs. In her enthusiasm she designed a cream-colored box labeled "The King's Eggs," illustrated with a brown egg and a chicken wearing a crown. She had several thousand boxes made up. Gable brought six hundred New Hampshire Red hens to put them in business, but the results were disastrous. Though Lombard often went out to the henhouse to sing the birds to sleep at night, they didn't lay with any profusion or regularity. The Gables abandoned the project when they discovered that production costs were averaging a dollar per egg.

Lombard was very proud, though, of the success they were having in raising the doves that she had originally sent to Gable after their meeting at The White Mayfair. The doves had now multiplied many times over and were kept in a large aviary at the ranch. Lombard saw the doves as a symbol of the love that was constantly growing between Gable and herself.

But Lombard's own efforts at perpetuating the Gable name were proving unsuccessful. Although there was one brief period of exaltation when she discovered she was pregnant, she found out at her next medical examination that she had miscarried, probably while horseback riding. Her doctor urged her, if she was really serious about having a baby, to avoid strenuous activity of any kind—to even consider taking a leave from her movie career.

Both were difficult decisions for Lombard to make at that time. She hated having to give up many of the outdoor activities Gable loved so much, and she could not drop out of films until she fulfilled her 1940 commitment to RKO for two pictures.

RKO was considering several projects for the motion-picture debut of Broadway's so-called "boy wonder," Orson Welles. When the studio offered Lombard the lead in one of those properties, "Smiler with a Knife," she turned it down because she had no desire to work with an untried director. Lombard claimed that if the picture was a flop, she'd be blamed for it, and if it was a hit, Welles would get all the credit. Welles went on to make "Citizen Kane" instead.

In the meantime there were more urgent problems. Gable was making "Boom Town," in which MGM's new European import, Hedy Lamarr, was a seductress trying to break up his marriage to Claudette Colbert. Though new to Hollywood, Lamarr already had a fast reputation as the result of appearing in the nude in "Ecstasy." Not trusting Gable around such a woman, Lombard made a surprise visit to the set while he was filming his love scene with Lamarr. According to one of the workers on the set, Lombard came on "looking like four million bucks," in a fur stole and ex-

pensive suit and hat. She had to prove that she could outclass
Lamarr, which really wasn't hard to do, even though Lamarr had
one of the most beautiful faces in the movies.

"Boom Town" was Gable's third and last film with Spencer
Tracy, who was now becoming too much of a box-office draw in
his own right for MGM to ever again use both Gable and Tracy in
one picture. While rehearsing for one of their fight scenes, Tracy
disappeared for a drink. Gable agreed to work with Tracy's
stand-in. Apparently carried away by suddenly being cast opposite
The King, the stand-in belted Gable so hard that he dropped to his
knees, his upper plate of false teeth broken and his lip split wide
open. Since "Boom Town" was nearly completed by that time,
there was no way of shooting around Gable while his teeth were
repaired and his lip healed. The delay added $50,000 to the cost of
the picture. Lombard told Gable that he was entitled more than
ever now to be called "the Toothless Wonder," the nickname having once been enviously pinned on Gable by Douglas Fairbanks
Senior, an earlier Hollywood "King."

Lombard's plan to make films at the same time as Gable didn't
always work out. As soon as he finished "Boom Town," she
started "They Knew What They Wanted." Directed by Garson
Kanin, the film version of Sidney Howard's play offered Lombard
one of her best dramatic roles, as the mail-order bride of Charles
Laughton. Lombard admired Laughton's talents, but detested him
as a person. She had it written into her contract that she would
never have to kiss him on his blubbery lips.

Laughton was a tyrant on the set, still living the Captain Bligh
character he'd played in Gable's "Mutiny on the Bounty." Garson
Kanin fought with Laughton constantly, with Lombard taking up
the slack in between bouts. She was always bawling out Laughton
in her saltiest language for slowing down production with his
temper tantrums.

Portions of "They Knew What They Wanted" were filmed
on location in the vineyards of the Napa Valley, north of San
Francisco. Lombard didn't like the idea of being separated from
Gable, so he went along on what amounted almost to a vacation for

them. They were put up in a private home, and they managed to work in some hunting and fishing when Lombard wasn't before the cameras. A few local residents even taught her how to stomp grapes with her bare feet.

When the Gables returned to the ranch, Lombard underwent another pregnancy test, which proved negative. She decided now that she would definitely take a year off from work as soon as her next picture was completed. Since Gable was due to return to MGM soon for another film, she hounded RKO into setting up her new vehicle as quickly as possible so that she would be working at the same time.

MGM liked the chemistry of Gable and Hedy Lamarr, quickly reuniting them in "Comrade X," an uninspired spinoff of Greta Garbo's "Ninotchka." In it Gable played a cynical newspaper reporter who falls in love with a Russian streetcar motorwoman. By this time Lombard had stopped worrying about competition from Hedy Lamarr, whose acting abilities were considered so minuscule that she was too occupied with turning in a decent performance to cast any eyes on Gable.

When Lombard discovered that Alfred Hitchcock was without an assignment at RKO at the time that she returned to comedy in her new film, "Mr. and Mrs. Smith," she coaxed him into directing the picture. The farce was hardly the suspense master's type of film, but he took it on out of his fondness for Lombard. The director had once created a storm in Hollywood by saying that actors were nothing more than cattle in his hands. On the opening day of "Mr. and Mrs. Smith," Hitchcock arrived on the set to find that Lombard had set up a corral with three live calves in it. One calf had an identification tag bearing Lombard's name, while the other two were labeled after her leading men, Robert Montgomery and Gene Raymond.

Hitchcock was famous for making a brief walk-on appearance in all of his pictures. Lombard insisted on directing that scene in "Mr. and Mrs. Smith," the one in which Hitchcock was supposed to be mistaken for a panhandler by Robert Montgomery and handed a dime. Lombard made Hitchcock do the scene over and over

again, to show him how it felt to be treated like cattle. Every time
he complained, she called the makeup man over to "powder Alfie's
nose."

Although Lombard enjoyed making the Hitchcock film, she
was relieved when it was finished. She could now devote herself
full time to being Mrs. Clark Gable, housewife and, hopefully,
mother.

As she started her year's leave, the duck-hunting season was
approaching. While Lombard had promised herself to cut down
on the strenuous outdoor life, she couldn't deny Gable the pleasure
of his favorite sport. The Gables again drove down to Baja California. When the duck hunting proved disappointing, they decided
to go higher up in the mountains to Laguna Hanson, where can-
vasbacks had been sighted.

Gable had telephoned MGM in Hollywood to arrange for
Paul Mantz, who had been the technical advisor on "Test Pilot," to
fly his twin-engine amphibian (which was nicknamed Nellie the
Goon) down to take them to Laguna Hanson. The duck hunting
was excellent, marred only by two mishaps for Lombard. She was
stung by a bee and developed a bad case of poison ivy rash. When
she returned home, she was confined to bed for several days, completely naked except for the white salve that covered her body
from head to toe.

Flying out of Laguna Hanson was more difficult than landing,
for the small lake was hemmed in by dense forest. The plane was
carrying a heavier load than usual, which caused Paul Mantz to
abort the first takeoff attempt. Some of the supplies had to be
removed before they could attempt another takeoff. This time it
was successful, though the plane narrowly missed the treetops.

Lombard, who was rarely afraid of anything, turned pale as
she observed their near mishap from the plane window. She said
to Gable, "Please, let's never travel in separate planes. Whenever I
fly, I want you with me."

The next time they traveled, right after Christmas 1940, the
Gables took the train. Their trip to Johns Hopkins Medical Center
in Baltimore had a twofold purpose. Gable was suffering intermit-

tent pain from an old shoulder injury sustained when a wall of
wooden bricks had caved in on him during the filming of "San
Francisco" in 1936. His own doctors had been unable to find the
source of Gable's complaints and recommended that he see a spe-
cialist at Johns Hopkins. Lombard decided to accompany him,
since the hospital was noted for its gynecology division. She hoped
they might be able to offer a solution to her childbearing problems.

At Johns Hopkins, the pain in Gable's shoulder was found to
be aggravated by the decaying stump of an old tooth, which was
promptly removed. Gable also had to undergo deep massage treatments for his shoulder, and was given a special series of exercises to
follow when he got home.

Lombard underwent a complete examination by the hospital's
chief gynecologist. The doctor could find nothing seriously wrong
with her, but suggested minor corrective surgery which would
improve her chances of conceiving. He recommended postponing
such an operation, however, until Lombard and Gable were definitely sure that their problem was not due to a lack of expertise in
their sexual relations. There was also the matter of Gable's own
potency to be considered before their failure to have a child could
be fixed on Lombard.

When the Gables checked out of Johns Hopkins, they decided to spend a few days in Washington, D.C., which Lombard
had never visited before. MGM's representative in the nation's
capital arranged for them to see all the major sights.

Hearing that Clark Gable and Carole Lombard were in the
city, President Roosevelt invited them to the White House to sit
in on a Fireside Chat, one of his periodic radio broadcasts to the
country on domestic and international issues.

The broadcast, on December 30, 1940, originated in the Oval
Room of the White House. Gable and Lombard sat in the front
row on wobbly gilt chairs, next to Secretary of State Cordell Hull
and the President's mother, Sara Delano Roosevelt. Watching the
President arrive in his rubber-tired wheelchair was something of
a shock to the Gables. FDR's disability had always been played
down in the press and the newsreels, out of fear that it would

lessen the public's confidence in him as the head of what was supposed to be the most powerful nation in the world.

FDR, who was just starting his third term in office, was trying to steer his country away from its isolationist policies into greater support of England and Russia in the war against Germany. That night, Gable and Lombard were eyewitnesses to one of FDR's most famous speeches, in which he envisioned the United States' role in the war as "the great arsenal of democracy."

FDR's talk confirmed Lombard's worst fears about the future when he said, "Never before has our American civilization been in such danger as now." He accused the Nazis of attempting "to dominate all life and thought in their own country . . . to enslave the whole of Europe . . . to use the resources of Europe to dominate the rest of the world."

The President said that "if Great Britain goes down, all of us in the Americas would be living at the point of a gun. The vast resources and wealth of this hemisphere constitute the most tempting loot in the world." FDR urged the country to step up its armament and defense efforts, hinting that the rationing of consumer and luxury goods might soon be necessary.

Despite the gravity of his speech, FDR was in a bright, sociable mood that night. Afterward, he and Eleanor Roosevelt chatted with Gable and Lombard for half an hour. The President, who was a movie enthusiast, questioned Gable closely about "Gone With the Wind," one of his favorite pictures, and complimented Lombard on her highly publicized support of the income-tax system.

The President was especially interested in getting the Gables' views on how the movie industry could help in the current emergency, particularly if it developed into a full-scale war. Lombard recalled the old World War I newsreels she'd seen of Mary Pickford and Charlie Chaplin selling bonds. She told FDR that he could count on the Gables performing the same kind of voluntary service, although she hoped that all-out war would somehow be averted.

twelve

Love and Marriage

Clark Gable and Carole Lombard celebrated their second wedding anniversary in March 1941. Lombard surprised Gable, who was making "They Met in Bombay" at the time, by staging a party on the set, catered by the Brown Derby. Everything in the way of refreshments and gifts was in pairs or doubles, to signify the Gables' two years of married life.

The Gable-Lombard marriage was fast becoming a legend. Counting their three-year affair, they had been together now for five years, refuting Hollywood's long-standing belief that couplings of movie stars couldn't last, because of the pressures of the business and the inevitable clashes of ego.

Gable and Lombard could succeed where others had failed because they were so well matched. They both had reached such heights in their careers that there was no reason for professional jealousy. In personality and temperament, they were synchronized opposites, Gable quiet and easygoing, Lombard boisterous and high-strung. As a couple, they struck a happy medium between the two extremes.

But most important, what really caused the marriage to be a success was Lombard's determination to make it so. Ever since childhood, she wanted to be the best and to have the best in everything. After she achieved that as an actress, she went after it in her personal life, setting her sights on one of the most desired men in the world and winning him. Their marriage had to work; otherwise Carole Lombard would be a loser for the first time in her life. She succeeded by turning herself into "a rough-and-ready pal" for Gable. As one friend said, "She was so vital, so full of the joy of living, that she carried everything and everybody along in her lighthearted wake. The atmosphere of love and companionship, the 'Clark comes first' attitude in all her thinking, had its effect on Clark. With Carole he began to relax, to be free, to shake off the old fears and depressions."

Yet remarkably, despite her subordinating herself to Gable, Carole Lombard never gave up her own identity or individuality.

In the 1941 census questionnaire, Lombard stated her occupation as "rancher's wife." She was not being flippant, for she was on leave from film-making to try to have a baby. She told her friends that if she became pregnant, she would give up her career entirely and devote herself full time to raising a family. There is no reason to doubt her sincerity. She had been at the top of her profession for almost six years, and there was no longer any great psychological or financial need for her to continue.

As the marriage entered its third year, the Gables started looking for a new home. As much as they enjoyed living on their twenty-acre enclave, they were finding it increasingly difficult to maintain any privacy. The location of their ranch was included in the maps of movie stars' homes that were sold to tourists along all the main thoroughfares of Hollywood. Sightseeing buses drove by several times a day. There were many instances of Gable fans, some of them elderly women, climbing the high chain-link fence to get a close look at their idol. The MGM police force often had to be called to remove them, although every effort had to be made to treat these intruders as gently as possible. The Gables' secretary kept a "crazy woman" file on all these incidents, in case they ever developed into lawsuits.

The Gables thought they could escape such annoyances by

moving much farther away from Hollywood. Their plan was to purchase a working cattle ranch of about a thousand acres, which would be self-sustaining. Since Lombard intended to stop acting once they started a family, Gable would commute back and forth to Hollywood for his film work.

Lombard went about the search for a new home with her usual enthusiasm. She started laying in food supplies even before they had the slightest idea of where they might be moving, and she bought ten king-sized garbage cans and filled them with dried beans. When her amazed secretary asked her why, Lombard said, "Pa loves his baked beans. We mustn't ever run short."

The Gables looked at ranches all over California, Oregon, Nevada and Arizona, even going as far as to put their present ranch up for sale, at an asking price of $85,000, or $35,000 more than they'd paid for it. But the prospect of selling the ranch, which had so many happy memories for her, saddened Lombard, and she refused to be there whenever an agent showed it. When Lombard heard that one of the prospective buyers had propositioned some of the servants to come to work for him, she made Gable take the ranch off the market. The Gables eventually abandoned their moving plans entirely as the threat of war increased.

Lombard had so removed herself from the Hollywood scene that she was being referred to in the fan magazines as "Gable's hermit wife." That was somewhat of a misnomer, for it implied that both she and Gable had become recluses, which was hardly the case. True, they did not mingle in café society, nor were they very close to any of their fellow stars. But they did have a large circle of friends whom they saw quite frequently. Gable's closest friend was Al Menasco, an automobile dealer, and Lombard remained very loyal to Fieldsie and her husband, director Walter Lang. Other close friends of the Gables included Howard Strickling, MGM's publicity chief; former actor Buster Collier, who had known Lombard from her earliest days in California; tennis champion Alice Marble, whose success was due in large part to Lombard's patronage; Norris Goff, the second half of the "Lum and Abner" radio team; Harry Fleischmann, owner of Gable's gun club; Phil Berg, Gable's agent; Eddie Mannix, Louis B. Mayer's second in command at MGM; and movie comedian Andy Devine.

Lombard also enjoyed a very close relationship with her mother, seeing her nearly every day, and her two brothers. Gable was fond of his mother-in-law, but barely tolerated Lombard's brothers, to whom she had been very generous over the years, even helping them to secure positions with a department store and a stock-brokerage house. Gable gave them short shrift, considering them spongers and hangers-on.

Because of her own tightly knit family circle, Lombard was always encouraging Gable to become closer to his father. Gable had been reconciled with the old man in the early Thirties, but they still didn't get along. Despite his son's success, the elder Gable could never accept acting as "real man's work." He kept reminding Gable that his movie salary was "just whistling and tobacco-chewing money" compared to what he could earn in the oil fields.

Gable supported his father, though not nearly so generously as Lombard did her mother, and this rather shabby treatment of his father disturbed Lombard. In the early part of 1941, she shamed Gable into building a house for the old man about five miles from the ranch. Gable's father seemed pleased with his new dwelling, but his relations with his son never improved very much as a result of it.

In his father's eyes, Gable could never do anything right. One weekend, Gable and Al Menasco were just finishing putting up a new fence at the ranch when Will Gable drove up in his dilapidated old Ford. Looking the job over, the elder Gable said to his son, "Now, kid, I taught you to build fences better than that." He made his "kid" and his friend take the whole fence down and nail it up again the right way. Lombard, who'd been superintending the building of the fence, shrieked with laughter over the whole episode.

Laughter had a lot to do with the success of the Gable-Lombard marriage. They both had a keen sense of humor; there was always a joke or a prank they could use to relieve any tensions that developed between them. When Gable went to open the barn door one morning, he was charged by an angry cow, which threw him halfway across the yard when he attempted to bulldog the animal Western fashion. Lombard went shopping later that day and bought him a red toreador's costume, which she solemnly presented to him at dinner.

Gable had to get even with her. She had just bought an expensive new riding outfit, especially designed by her costume-designer friend Irene. Gable said Lombard deserved a new horse to go with it, promising her that a thoroughbred would be delivered in the morning. When she raced out of the house the next day to see it, Lombard was confronted with a decrepit, swaybacked horse that, like herself, was a veteran of the old Mack Sennett comedies. Gable had rented it for the day.

But like all marriages, Gable and Lombard's had its unavoidable moments of crisis, given Gable's status as the preeminent romantic idol of his day. Women of all ages were constantly making overtures to him, especially at the studio. His powers of resistance being virtually nil, he sometimes found himself in trouble with Lombard when she discovered his latest escapades.

For a woman of that time, Lombard had a remarkably liberal attitude towards Gable's affairs. As long as they did not pose a serious threat to the marriage, she let many of them pass. She could not envision Gable becoming deeply involved with any of the starlets, extra players and secretaries who generally made themselves available. Lombard had been around the movie studios long enough herself to know that these sudden infatuations were unavoidable, that Gable's succumbing to them was entirely a physical response, and that they meant no lessening of his love for her.

But Lombard's liberalism did not extend to Gable's leading ladies, especially when they were blondes and reputed to be free and easy in their romantic attachments. In the summer of 1941, she battled with Gable over Lana Turner, who was starring opposite him in "Honky Tonk."

Lana Turner was then twenty-one, eleven years younger than Lombard and nineteen years younger than Gable. The physical interaction between this voluptuous girl and a mature man like Gable was predictable, and was bound to incite a violent reaction from his jealous wife.

As soon as production started on "Honky Tonk," Hollywood was rife with rumors that Lana Turner was after Gable, that she was bragging to friends that she was going to break up his marriage to Carole Lombard. At one point the situation became so tense that Lombard reportedly complained to Louis B. Mayer, threatening to pull her husband off the picture unless Turner was told that Gable was off limits. Whether this really happened is doubtful, since Lombard was not the type to ask others to fight her battles for her. She directed her attack on Gable himself, making it painfully clear to him how she would take care of both him and Lana Turner if she ever caught them together.

Lombard visited the set of "Honky Tonk" far more frequently than she had any of Gable's other films and tried to be there whenever he was filming a love scene with Lana Turner. A technician working on the film said that Gable, sensing that Lombard was there, reddened at the neckline, and that her purpose was to make him uneasy. Once, when a scene was completed, Lombard snapped rather sarcastically at Turner, "Don't mind me, Lana. I know you must be having a tough time. Pappy's not very good in a clinch." Gable was terribly embarrassed and in a testy mood for days afterward.

The commotion over Lana Turner subsided when Gable finished the film. The Gables patched things up by making a fishing trip to the Rogue River in Oregon, but their stay at the We-Ask-U Inn hunting lodge was marred by hordes of rowdy teen-agers who surrounded their cabin and rapped on the windows all night. Packing up and driving all the way to Lake Meade, Nevada, the Gables hired a cabin cruiser and were able to protect their privacy by not touching shore for several days.

The Gables' life together was now about equally divided between the ranch and frequent hunting and fishing trips. For two Hollywood movie stars, it was an unglamorous existence. But neither Gable nor Lombard had ever been happier.

Except for their hunting trips, they rarely went anywhere. "We die if we have to go out of an evening," Lombard once said. When they were alone, they played showdown poker or back-gammon, for penny stakes. They read a great deal, Lombard devouring a surprisingly wide variety of books, usually with an eye to whether they might make a good film for herself or her husband. Gable stuck to mystery novels.

Occasionally Lombard would stage what she called a "fun party" for their friends and some of the stars and executives they worked with at the studios. The parties were never as lavish or screwy as the ones Lombard used to throw before she met Gable, but there was usually a gimmick involved. One night the guests arrived to find the Gables' patio set up for a twelve-piece orchestra, with all the necessary instruments and music stands. The hitch was that there were no musicians. Lombard urged guests to pick up their preferred instruments and form a band. Gable sat in on drums, Fred MacMurray on saxophone, Buster Collier at the piano. Spencer Tracy played bass, while Robert Taylor and Dick Powell joined the brass section. Lombard took up the trumpet and also made an at-tempt at being the band's leader.

Late one afternoon, the Gables were sitting alone on the patio, watching the sun go down. Feeling rather heady after several Scotches, Gable said, "Ma, we're lucky people. We've got this ranch, and while it's not going to support us, it feels like a ranch, it smells and looks like a ranch. It's not just animals and hay. We've got the house fixed just to suit us, we've both got good jobs, friends, money in the bank and our health. God's been good to us. Can you think of anything you really want that you haven't got?"

Lombard sipped on her Coca-Cola before she answered. "Pa, to tell you the truth, I could use a couple of loads of manure if we're going to do any good with those fruit trees."

The one thing that Lombard did want was not a joking matter.

Despite recurrent rumors in the newspapers that the Gables were expecting "a little Rhett Butler or possibly a Rhetta," Lombard's attempts at having a baby were proving futile. In the fall of 1941, as she approached the end of her year's leave from film-making, she grew increasingly depressed at her apparent failure to become pregnant. With her mother's encouragement, she began taking an interest in religion, hoping that she might find some spiritual solace for her inner anguish. Her mother, whose fascination with the occult extended to metaphysics and Eastern religions, was active in the Bahai Church and the Church of Religious Science.

This spiritual side of Carole Lombard was something few people knew about. Writer Adela Rogers St. Johns, who'd been a close friend of Gable's since his early days at MGM, discovered it one day when she visited the ranch. Gable was off looking at a horse, so Lombard sat and chatted with St. Johns in the back yard while they waited for his return.

Quite unexpectedly, Lombard asked the visitor, "Look, do you believe in God? I don't mean an old guy with long spinach on his chin. I mean something for every day—wherever you are?" When St. Johns said she did believe, Lombard continued, "Do you get solemn about it? I don't, and some people might not understand. That's why I never talk about it. I think it's all here—in the mountains and the desert. I don't think God is a softie, either. In the end it's better if people are forced back into—well—being right, before they're too far gone. I think your temple is your everyday living."

Lombard spoke of her great desire to have children. She still hadn't completely given up hope. "I never can see into the future at all," Lombard said. "I guess I'm too busy living every day, or something. Look—I'm not afraid of growing old. I think it's wonderful. Look at my mother, Bessie. She's nine times the woman I am. It sounds sort of nice. When you're out of all the tailspins of youth, when you're content, like Clark and I are, and have learned not to let emotional high blood pressure hit a boiling point and knock you all silly, then you begin to enjoy everything. So much you missed when you were skittering around as a kid.

"But I never see myself growing old," Lombard said. "I don't have any pictures of how I'll look or what I'll do. I can see myself with a little baby, but not with a baby grown up."

Lombard did not seem distressed when she made that statement. She said it simply, a little quizzically, but apparently with no sense of premonition or foreboding. She continued, "I like it when the going is tough. If you wait for everything to be just right in your life, you'll never get any happiness. You have to fight for it and get it anyway. The minute you start fighting for anything, you've won. The end doesn't matter.

"We're so dumb we maybe don't even know what the end is," Lombard said. "There's got to be something after this—after this life—where you can use all you've learned here, or nothing makes any sense. . . . When you're in there fighting, you always feel so clean. Ugly things drop away. I guess God never lost a fight. The only time you're a cinch to lose is when you won't fight for what you believe in."

But all the fighting in the world wasn't going to help Lombard become a mother. For the first time in her life she had to admit defeat—at least temporarily. She and Gable decided that the best thing for her to do was to return to work, which would put her mind on other things and help her out of her depression.

Producer Alexander Korda was preparing a new Ernst Lubitsch film, "To Be or Not to Be," which was to star Jack Benny and Miriam Hopkins. Benny was not happy with the prospect of working with Hopkins, who was very temperamental. When he heard that Carole Lombard was shopping around for a film, Benny persuaded Korda and Lubitsch to offer her the part. Lombard liked the script, a comedy with a timely anti-Nazi theme. She signed for the picture after negotiating an advantageous deal for herself that included a percentage of the profits and gave her top billing over Jack Benny. The comedian's agent objected to the billing, but Benny told him, "Pictures are her business, radio's mine. Let her name come first."

The making of "To Be or Not to Be" violated Lombard's pledge to work only when Gable did. With "Honky Tonk," the picture he'd made with Lana Turner, he had completed his commitments for 1941. With the duck and pheasant season about to start, Gable was somewhat put out by Lombard's not being able to go with him, so before she started filming, she managed to squeeze in a few days to go hunting with Gable in South Dakota. It was to be their last trip together.

thirteen

Lombard's Last Mission

December 7, 1941, was a sunny, sparkling Sunday in the San Fernando Valley, with the temperature in the 80s. Carole Lombard slept late that morning—it was her one day off during the week from "To Be or Not to Be"—but she was breakfasting by the time the news of the Japanese sneak attack on Pearl Harbor flashed over the radio at 11:26 A.M. Although details were still incomplete, hundreds, perhaps thousands, of American lives were believed lost. When she heard the bulletin, Lombard broke into tears and ran looking for Gable, who was out in the stable grooming the horses.

Ardent patriot that she was, Lombard was terribly upset, much more so than Gable when she told him the news. Right away, she shook her fist in the air, and vowed to go to the Pacific and kill "Japs" with her bare hands. Gable took her back into the house, where they spent most of the day listening to the descriptions of the tragic events of Pearl Harbor as they became known. Lombard herself was scheduled to be on the radio that afternoon, making a guest appearance on Jack Benny's show. But this being no time for comedy, she soon received a phone call that the program was postponed to a later date.

Lombard's first thought was of how she and Gable could help in the emergency, which the radio bulletins indicated would probably turn into full-scale war with Japan within twenty-four hours. Remembering their visit with President Roosevelt that previous January, Lombard told Gable that they must write to him as soon as possible, renewing their pledge to help in the war effort. They framed a letter to FDR, which Gable dictated to their secretary and sent off the next morning.

Lombard, who was always the thinker in the Gable family, had already worked out a plan in her mind about their roles in the war effort. She thought that Gable should enlist in the military service and that she would join the Red Cross or perhaps one of the women's branches of the Army or Navy.

It took a lot of persuading to bring Gable around to her way of thinking. Soon to celebrate his forty-first birthday, Gable was really too old to be a soldier. And after all the years it had taken him to achieve his present success, he wasn't about to give up his exceedingly comfortable existence or his $7,500-a-week salary. There were to be many arguments between Gable and Lombard over this in the weeks to come.

When Lombard returned to work the day after Pearl Harbor, she found that Hollywood had started its own defense efforts. Members of the State Guard had been posted at the studios' water towers, laboratories and technical departments, as a precaution against sabotage. All Japanese employees—there were quite a few working as gardeners, handymen and wardrobe-department seamstresses—were barred from entering the studios until the Government adopted an official policy toward Japanese nationals.

Lombard was so off her usual carefree mood during that day's filming of "To Be or Not to Be" that she didn't even bother to tease Jack Benny about his effeminate walk or call him "Auntie," as she usually did. Production was halted twice that day because of the national emergency. In the morning, a State Guard officer came on the set and ordered ten extras to report for duty immediately. A little later, all work stopped as President Roosevelt came on the radio. Describing December 7, 1941, as "a date which will live in infamy," he said, "Always will our whole nation remember the character of the onslaught against us. No matter how long it may take us to overcome this premeditated invasion, the American people in their righteous might will win through to absolute victory." Though she knew there was no other choice, Lombard's heart sank when FDR said that he had asked Congress to declare a state of war. She hurried home to Gable that night full of fears for their future.

Despite his involvement in the world crisis, President Roosevelt somehow managed to answer the letter that the Gables had sent him right after Pearl Harbor; about a week later, they received a short but gracious note from FDR, thanking them for offering their help. But much to Lombard's disappointment, the President said that for the time being, both she and Gable could best serve their country by continuing to appear in films, describing how important entertainment was to building public morale in time of war. "You are needed where you are," FDR told the Gables.

Lombard, who generally agreed with the President's pronouncements, thought he was wrong this time. She still kept after Gable about going into the service, but soon found that she had not only her husband to do battle with, but also MGM. The studio's stars were its most important asset and Louis B. Mayer had no intention of losing them to the war effort if he could help it. MGM was already appealing Mickey Rooney's 1-A draft classification, on the basis of essentiality. Since Gable was way above draft age, he could only enter the service voluntarily. MGM did not look favorably on releasing its biggest star from his contract to risk his life defending his country.

But Lombard was merciless in her badgering of Gable. She finally broke him down to the point where he said he would enlist if MGM approved. Horrified, Mayer arranged a meeting for Gable with Lowell Mellett, whom President Roosevelt had appointed as his wartime liaison with the motion picture industry. Mellett told Gable almost the same thing that FDR had in his letter, that his real job was to provide entertainment, keep up morale and pay his gigantic taxes. Later, Mellett told columnist Walter Winchell,

"Gable's one of the people's daily habits. We don't want to rob them of their steady habits all at once. That's the one thing we've copied from Goebbels' propaganda machine."

To further strengthen its hold on Gable, MGM assigned him to a new picture, "Somewhere I'll Find You," which was to start production early in 1942. This development angered Lombard, especially when she learned that Lana Turner was again going to be Gable's co-star.

Lombard had considered making "To Be or Not to Be" her last picture for the duration of the war. But now that Gable was locked in for at least a couple of months, she signed on for just one more picture, Columbia's "They All Kissed the Bride." The film was scheduled to begin shortly after Gable's, and Lombard hoped that when they were both finished, they would be able to devote themselves full time to the war effort.

In the meantime, Lombard was able to do her bit by participating with Gable in the activities of the Hollywood Victory Committee, an organization that had been set up three days after Pearl Harbor to enlist the movie industry's help in entertaining the armed forces and in supporting the war effort. Gable, because of his reputation as "The King," was the logical choice to serve as chairman of the Screen Actors Division. Knowing how it would please Lombard, he accepted the nomination.

The first meeting of the actors' group at the Beverly Wilshire Hotel on December 22, 1941, might have been mistaken for a movie premiere, had these not already been banned for the duration of the war. Most of the women, including Carole Lombard, wore expensive fur coats and the elaborate hats that were one of the last vestiges of prewar Hollywood. Lombard also wore a black silk dress and told everyone that she was disguised as a blackout.

Lombard beamed with pride when Gable addressed the large group of stars and actors, outlining the goals of the Hollywood Victory Committee and urging everyone to volunteer their services. A committee of fifteen, headed by Gable, was chosen to coordinate talent for bond rallies, camp shows and hospital tours. Serving with Gable on the committee were Myrna Loy, Claudette Colbert,

Charles Boyer, Bob Hope, Rosalind Russell, John Garfield, Bette Davis, Tyrone Power, Gary Cooper, Ginger Rogers, Ronald Colman, Cary Grant, Irene Dunne and Jack Benny. Carole Lombard, as the chairman's wife, was the first one to stand up and pledge her cooperation. She was quickly seconded by Marlene Dietrich, Jeanette MacDonald, Henry Fonda, George Raft, Merle Oberon, Rudy Vallee, Carole Landis and Kay Kayser.

The meeting was so successful that the Gables celebrated afterward by making a rare night out of it at Ciro's nightclub. But before they could enter, they had to make a stop at a bookstore. No one, not even Clark Gable and Carole Lombard, was being admitted to Ciro's that night without first donating a book for hospitalized servicemen.

"To Be or Not to Be" completed filming on Christmas Eve. At the celebration party on the set, Lombard displayed her usual generosity, doling out presents to all the crew, including a kitten to the wardrobe woman and twenty-five pounds of licorice drops to an assistant director who'd been stealing from her own supply of candy throughout production.

Lombard left the party early, shouting, "Goodbye, fellows. I've had a swell time, but Clark and I have a more important job to do now. We're going to entertain a bunch of soldiers for Christmas." She then drove to MGM, where the studio had arranged a holiday entertainment for servicemen, with Gable as the host.

The Gables' own Christmas celebration was very conservative that year. While Lombard usually decorated the house lavishly and spent weeks shopping for gifts, this time she had cut back drastically because of the war. Most of the people on the Gables' gift list received a simple card indicating that a donation had been made in their name to the Red Cross.

The Gables did not stint, however, on the gifts they presented to each other. Gable gave Lombard a pair of ruby-and-diamond clips to match her ruby heart. Lombard's gift to him was an ultra-slim gold cigarette case, inscribed "Pa, Dear—I love you—Ma."

But that Christmas had little meaning for the Gables as the war news continued to be grim. Wake Island and Hong Kong had fallen to the Japanese. London was under heavy bombardment by the Germans. Closer to home, there was a growing fear that the Japanese would soon launch a sneak attack on the Pacific Coast. Air-raid drills were being held with increasing regularity. The Gables made their horses available for the mounted squadron of air-raid wardens that was patrolling the San Fernando Valley.

Lombard saw a greater need than ever for Gable to go into the service and there was now the possibility that he eventually could be drafted. Just before Christmas, Congress had passed a new draft bill, requiring all men between eighteen and sixty-four to register although, for the time being, only those from twenty to forty-four were actually eligible for the draft, with the youngest men to be called first.

Realizing that any attempt to keep Gable out of the service now would be futile and cause embarrassment for all concerned, MGM tried to persuade him to go in as a commissioned officer. The studio, which did not approve of "The King of Hollywood" being drafted, was sure it could use its considerable influence in Washington to get him a posh desk job far from the sound of battle.

Lombard became enraged when told of this latest development, saying the last thing she wanted for Gable was "one of those phony commissions." She thought he should set an example for the rest of the country by going in as an ordinary private.

New Year's Eve, 1941, was hardly a time to be joyous. The Gables spent it quietly, realizing that it might well be their last together for a long time to come. They were certain that they would be separated by the war, and prayed that the separation would not be a long one.

At the beginning of 1942, while he was waiting to start his next film, Gable was devoting some of his time to the chairmanship of the talent-coordinating division of the Hollywood Victory Committee. One of the first requests received was to send a film star to Indiana to help promote the launching of the state's campaign to sell U.S. Defense Bonds.

Gable was to regret his next move for the rest of his life. He nominated his own wife for the tour. Since Lombard was a native of Indiana, he was sure she would be delighted to return to her home state for this patriotic mission.

Lombard, who was thoroughly disgusted with herself over the little she had done so far for the war effort, was even more thrilled by the prospect of the tour than Gable had imagined. Although she really would have liked to be on the front lines taking potshots at the enemy with her Springfield 306, the bond tour would at least give her a chance to burn up some of that energy while doing something positive for her country.

Lombard wanted Gable to go with her. Since this was impossible because of his commitment for "Somewhere I'll Find You," Gable suggested that Lombard take her mother along in his place. Mrs. Peters, who hadn't been back to Indiana for many years, gratefully accepted the invitation to accompany her daughter.

Lombard went about preparing for the tour as if she were starting a new picture. She gave her designer friend Irene a rush order for some new clothes. In deference to those grim times, everything was to be in black—a trim street dress for daytime wear and a strapless velvet gown for evenings. Lombard also bought a whole new outfit for her mother.

Gable asked MGM's publicity department to prepare a few speeches for Lombard to deliver along her tour route. Though her final destination was Indianapolis, she was to take the train and make brief stops in Salt Lake City, Chicago and other points along the way. At each stop, she was to give a few press interviews and a platform speech in support of defense bonds.

Cornwell Jackson, one of Gable's agents, had once lived in Indianapolis, and he offered to accompany Lombard and her mother on the tour. When he was unable to go, due to sudden business complications, Gable persuaded Otto Winkler to take his place. Winkler was very busy with his own work at MGM, but he had been so involved in the Gables' lives since the time of their wedding that he couldn't very well refuse.

For all her eagerness to get started and to prove what a supersaleswoman she could be, Lombard was not keen on leaving Gable alone. She was apprehensive about his working again with

Lana Turner. And to add to her concern, Lombard had reason to believe that Gable was playing fast and loose with another young actress at MGM. Shortly before she was to leave, Lombard battled fiercely with Gable over this entire situation.

Gable did not see his wife off when she left on her bond tour from Los Angeles' Union Station on January 12, 1942. MGM excused his absence by stating that he'd flown to Washington for meetings with military officials on his service future and couldn't get back in time for Lombard's departure. But there are indications that he was missing for a more personal reason—that he had lost his temper and walked out on Lombard after their quarrel over his flings with other women.

Whatever the reason for Gable's absence, Lombard was very upset as she made her final preparations to leave. She handed their secretary, Jean Garceau, a series of notes she had written for Gable, with instructions to give him one for each of the days she was to be away. Just before she left the house, Lombard hugged the secretary and said, "Take care of my old man for me, will you, Jeanie? You know you'll be working with him more and more now." Garceau said later that Lombard "left on a very quiet and rather sad note—which was unlike her, usually so gay and lighthearted."

Gable returned home, from wherever he had been, the day after Lombard left. She called him constantly from every stop along her route. Apparently, if they'd had a rift, they managed to patch up their differences over the phone. This explained why she was so anxious to get home once the tour was finished.

Despite freezing weather, Lombard attracted large crowds wherever she stopped. From Ogden, Utah, she cabled her secretary: "Know it is peaceful without me. Know you will have nothing to do. Ha Ha. Killed them at Salt Lake. Ten below." At one point, Lombard got so carried away by her own patriotic campaigning that she wired Gable, "Hey Pappy. You better get into this man's Army."

Lombard, her mother and Otto Winkler reached Indianapolis on the morning of January 15 and were rushed by motorcade to the east lawn of the State House for a flag-raising ceremony. The flag was the same one that had flown over the national Capitol the day the United States declared war against Japan. As the flag was raised, Lombard lifted her hand in the V for Victory sign and shouted, "Heads up, hands up, America! Let's give a cheer that will be heard in Tokyo and Berlin."

Three thousand people were lined up in the lobby of the State House waiting to buy bonds from Lombard. She gave each purchaser a receipt that carried her autographed picture and the message, "Thank you for joining with me in this vital crusade to make America strong." As people surged by giving her their orders for bonds, Lombard yelled, "I'm like a barker at a carnival." When anyone showed the slightest sales resistance, she said, "If my husband was here, you'd buy, I betcha."

Will H. Hays, the movie czar who'd once complained so bitterly about Gable and Lombard's involvement in the "Unmarried Husbands and Wives" fracas, was another native Hoosier participating in the bond drive. He had nothing but admiration for Lombard now. He was so impressed by the crowd's reaction to Lombard at the mass meeting that night that he was moved to state later, "It felt like an old-time political rally, and I thought what a joy it would be to any campaign manager to have such a candidate as this evening's star. She was the first principal I had ever seen go through such an occasion with never a single mistake. Every time there was anything to be said or done, she said or did exactly the right thing. Her observations were all appropriate and at times absolutely brilliant. It was ad libbing at its best. At no time was there the slightest tinge of acting."

Carole Lombard's final public appearance, on the stage of Cadle Tabernacle that night of January 15, 1942, must have been a moving experience for an audience in those war-nerved times. Three military bands and a color guard presented a patriotic pageant. The Lord's Prayer was sung by an all-black chorus. By the time Lombard appeared in her strapless evening gown, the crowd was wildly enthusiastic. As the audience joined her in singing "The Star Spangled Banner," backed by three bands and the Tabernacle pipe organ, she was overcome by the excitement and broke into tears.

Afterward, Will Hays told Lombard that he was going to wire Gable how well she had carried out her mission. She said, "Good! Give the old boy a shot, it'll do him good." Hays sent Gable the following telegram: "Great day here. Carole was perfect. Really she was magnificent. They sold in this one day $2,017,513 worth of bonds, with a quota of only $500,000. Everyone deeply grateful."

Lombard's last-minute decision to fly home instead of taking the train forced her to cancel bond-promoting stops she had intended to make in Kansas City and Albuquerque on the way back. She told the Government officials responsible for her tour that she would make it up to them another time.

That was one promise Carole Lombard never kept. She died less than twenty-four hours later in the crash of the plane that was taking her home to Clark Gable.

fourteen

A Nation Mourns

It was three days before the remains of the bodies were brought down from the crash site atop Table Rock Mountain. The descent over frozen trails was so treacherous that at one point a pack horse and its canvas-wrapped burden of cadavers slipped and plunged off a cliff.

Carole Lombard's remains were among the first to be retrieved. But Clark Gable refused to leave Las Vegas until those of Lombard's mother and Otto Winkler had also been turned over to him. Gable went alone to a local mortuary to select the caskets in which the three bodies would be taken back to Los Angeles. Afterward, he went to the temporary headquarters of the rescue operation and helped to serve food to the returning men. Taking pity on a toothless old cowboy trying to gum his way through a steak, Gable handed a deputy sheriff a hundred-dollar bill and told him, "For God's sake, buy that guy some teeth."

In the meantime, Carole Lombard's death was being treated as a national tragedy. President Roosevelt sent Gable the following telegram: "Mrs. Roosevelt and I are deeply distressed. Carole was our friend, our guest in happier days. She brought great joy to all who knew her and to millions who knew her only as a great artist. She gave unselfishly of her time and talent to serve her government in peace and in war. She loved her country. She is and always will be a star, one we shall never forget nor cease to be grateful to. Deepest sympathy."

Later, FDR awarded Carole Lombard a medal as "The first woman to be killed in action in the defense of her country in its war against the Axis powers."

In Hollywood, on January 19, all activities at the movie studios were halted at noon as Taps was sounded and a short tribute was paid to Lombard. In Washington, the United States Senate paused to hear a tribute from Senator Willis of Lombard's home state of Indiana.

One person, however, thought Lombard's death was receiving more attention than it was due. CBS radio commentator Elmer Davis, then one of the most influential men in the country, said on the air, "If you judge from the newspaper headlines of the past two days, this is still a country where the death of a movie actress is more important than the death of fifteen Army fliers in the same accident. Fortunately there is plenty of evidence that, in this instance, the newspaper headlines misrepresent the feeling of the public. Certainly an immense number of Americans have come to realize by now with the sort of times we live in that the death of an artist, however distinguished and popular, is of less importance to the future of the nation than the loss of fifteen of the highly trained men on whom we must depend for victory."

Davis' comments brought a quick rebuttal from Walter Winchell, who snapped, "I expect we can train 15 more pilots, dreadful as their loss was. I expect we can find other ways to sell more than $2,000,000 in defense bonds in one day. But you could dredge Hollywood from end to end and not find another girl who could get out there and sell that many that fast solo."

The presence of the fifteen pilots on the plane set off considerable speculation during those early days of World War II as to whether the crash might have been caused by enemy sabotage. Right after the accident, a military guard covered the wreckage until an investigation by the Civil Aeronautics Board was completed. The CAB's final report, however, ruled out sabotage, placing the cause of the crash on "the failure of the captain after departure from Las Vegas to follow the proper course by making use of the navigational facilities available to him." In other words, pilot error.

But there was always to be an undercurrent of suspicion that sabotage was indeed involved, that the Government could not risk its exposure. The United States was suffering such severe war losses at that time that admission of an enemy success on home ground might have seriously undermined public morale.

As soon as he took custody of the three bodies, Gable began his sad journey home by train, accompanying the caskets that were placed in the baggage car. Since the Las Vegas terminal was packed with reporters and photographers trying to get at the grieving "King," Gable was sneaked into his drawing room on the train from the opposite side of the platform. To avoid a similar scene in Los Angeles, Gable and his cargo left the train a stop ahead at Colton, where MGM representatives were waiting for him with a limousine, while an ambulance stood by to take the caskets to the mortuary at Forest Lawn. Gable, too overcome by sorrow to return immediately to the ranch, was taken to the home of his friend, Al Menasco, in San Gabriel.

Since Carole Lombard had been on a patriotic mission, the U.S. Defense Department wanted to give her a full military funeral. At an Army encampment in Griffith Park, a rifle squad and detachment of men were already being drilled for the funeral services. Within Hollywood itself, many of Lombard's friends and former co-workers were talking of erecting a gigantic mausoleum in her honor.

Lombard had specified in her will exactly how she wanted her funeral to be conducted, as a precaution against its being turned into a public spectacle, as her friend Jean Harlow's had been. She had requested that it be as simple as possible, limited to family and very close friends, and had outlined the order of the funeral service and the texts that were to be read. She had even requested to be buried in a white gown designed by Irene.

Out of respect for his wife's wishes, Gable asked the Army to cancel its offer of a military funeral. He proceeded to make all the arrangements exactly as Lombard had requested, with one alteration that she could not have anticipated at the time she drew up her will: It was to be a double funeral, for Carole Lombard and her mother, Elizabeth Peters.

The services were held at the Church of the Recessional at Forest Lawn on January 21, 1942, five days after the plane crash. In keeping with Lombard's request, the public and photographers were barred, although a few reporters were admitted. There were only forty-six mourners in the chapel, which seated one hundred and fifty, and all were relatives or friends. Few, except for William Powell, Spencer Tracy, Myrna Loy, Jack Benny and Fred Mac-Murray, were stars.

Clark Gable sat in a private family room, together with his father, Lombard's brothers and Mrs. Peters' three sisters. The dark-gray steel coffins of Lombard and her mother were closed and covered by sweeping blankets of gardenias and orchids.

The services were conducted by a Methodist minister, who, faithfully following the instructions that Lombard had left in her will, read from the fourteenth chapter of John and the Twenty-third Psalm. He then recited a short poem that had been a favorite of Lombard and her mother's:

> *The dark threads are as needful*
> *In the Weaver's skillful hand,*
> *As the threads of gold and silver*
> *In the pattern He has planned.*

The service concluded with a two-sentence quotation from the Persian philosopher Baha'u'llah: "I have made death even as glad tidings unto thee. Why dost thou mourn at its approach?"

Gable sat solemnly through the service, his eyes shielded by dark glasses. After the burial at Forest Lawn, he returned with a few friends to the ranch for the first time since Lombard's death. Their secretary, who still had one last note that Lombard had left Gable before she departed on her bond tour, felt he should have it.

When Gable read whatever was contained in those final words from his dead wife, he broke down and cried. "Up until this time," secretary Jean Garceau said later, "Clark had borne himself with fortitude and courage, had been stronger than any of us throughout the entire ordeal. . . . After that Clark was in perfect control, his grief masked. He asked no sympathy, wanted none, was unapproachable."

The day after the funeral of Lombard and her mother, services were held for Otto Winkler, the MGM press agent who had died with them. Gable felt very guilty over his friend's death, since he had asked Winkler to accompany Lombard as a personal favor to him, and he escorted Winkler's widow to the funeral. Gable promised Mrs. Winkler that he would do everything he could to provide for her future.

Since Gable was in no emotional condition to go back to work in the ironically titled "Somewhere I'll Find You," the film he had just started when Lombard was killed, MGM shut down production for a month while he tried to adjust to the impact of the tragedy.

Lombard's death was also having its effect on two other films. The release of her last picture, "To Be or Not to Be," was postponed, to allow a suitable period of mourning. Director Ernst Lubitsch cut a line of dialogue from the film, in which Lombard jokingly asked Jack Benny, "What can happen in a plane?" Benny personally was taking Lombard's death very hard. When he first heard the news of her death on the radio, he hurried into his car to drive to Las Vegas. After ten miles, Benny turned back, realizing how senseless it was.

"They All Kissed the Bride," which was supposed to be Carole Lombard's next picture, got Joan Crawford as the new leading lady. She took over Lombard's part with the understanding that all of her $112,500 salary would go to the Red Cross and other wartime charities. Crawford's agent was not as benevolent as she was. When he tried to deduct his 10 percent commission from the money that was to go to charity, she fired him. The fact that Joan Crawford and Clark Gable had once been lovers was not lost on Hollywood gossips, who interpreted her taking over Lombard's role as a first step toward getting Gable back, now that he was free. Associates said that Crawford had always regretted turning Gable down when he offered to marry her in the early Thirties.

With "Somewhere I'll Find You" temporarily suspended, Gable went off to the Rogue River in Oregon for a couple of weeks with his long-time hunting friend Harry Fleischmann. But the change didn't help. Returning to the ranch, Gable was still in a state of shock and disbelief over his wife's death. When friends came to call, he often spoke of Lombard as if she were still alive and he was expecting her home at any moment.

Since Lombard's death, Gable had lost twenty pounds and was so hypertense that his doctor would not permit him to drink anything stronger than white wine. Gable spent hours roaming the ranch alone. He sat in the garden, staring at the shrubs and trees that Lombard had planted. He walked to the stables to calm her horse, Melody, who had turned very fidgety in her mistress' absence. Prior to Lombard's death, her little dachshund, Commissioner, had been so devoted to Lombard that he would never go near Gable. Now, Commissioner was constantly at Gable's side.

Gable's walks usually took him to the garage, where he would sit silently in the Dodge station wagon that he and Lombard had used on so many of their hunting trips. He never drove it again after her death, but always maintained it in immaculate condition.

Gable had given the servants strict instructions to keep Lombard's bedroom suite exactly as she had left it. When they cleaned, every bottle on her dressing table, every piece of clothing in her closets, had to be put back in the same place. Even a book that Lombard had been reading, *The Cloud of the Unknowing*, was left open to the page she had marked.

But for all his sadness, Gable managed to display his usual concern over money when it came to settling Lombard's estate. Clothes that she had purchased from her wardrobe in "To Be or Not to Be" were returned to the studio for a full refund. Although it was reported that Gable had waived his right to sue TWA over his wife's death so that Otto Winkler's widow could obtain a better settlement from the airline, Gable did nothing of the kind. He got Mrs. Winkler to waive *her* rights, with the promise that he would build her a house and establish a $100,000 annuity for her. Years later, Mrs. Winkler was to sue Gable, claiming that he had reneged on his promise and had given her a house worth only $7,500.

Everything that Lombard had went to Gable, with the exception of the annuities she left to her friend Fieldsie Lang and to her mother. The latter was divided equally between Lombard's two brothers, who had been well taken care of by Lombard during her lifetime but resented Gable's inheriting her entire estate. Gable, who never had much use for his brothers-in-law, refused to have anything to do with them after the funeral.

For a star who had been one of the highest paid in Hollywood, Lombard's estate was not that large. The tax appraiser fixed its value at $300,000, not including the ranch, which, though paid for by Lombard, was registered in Gable's name, or the percentage interest that she had in her last five pictures.

For a time after his wife's death, Gable talked of selling the ranch. He looked at homes in Bel-Air and Beverly Hills, and even considered buying Greta Garbo's former house in Brentwood. But his friends never took his intentions very seriously, knowing he could never break away from the home that was so pervaded by Carole Lombard's spirit.

Before Gable would return to work, he insisted that MGM find a new title for "Somewhere I'll Find You," which was unpleasantly close to his personal dilemma. "I couldn't walk on a set with those words before me," Gable said. MGM changed the title to "Red Light," but reverted to the original "Somewhere I'll Find You" when the picture was released later in the year. The studio wasn't about to give up a surefire title like that.

On Gable's first morning back, the cast and crew were very nervous, not knowing what to expect of him. Yet, as one observer commented, "If you didn't look closely and ignored his thinness, he was the usual Gable, with the flashing smile and the jaunty wisecracks." Gable's only deviation from his normal routine was at lunchtime. He had always eaten at the directors' and writers' table in the main dining room or at the counter with some of the crew. Now he retired to his dressing room and ate alone.

Lana Turner, his leading lady, was keeping a respectful distance. Though she was generally very frolicsome on the set, she stayed in her dressing room most of the time. When she had a scene with Gable, she tried to be sympathetic without being maudlin. Asked by a reporter what it was like working with the widower, Turner said, "I've never known anyone to suffer so much. It breaks my heart to see him try to pull himself together before every scene. Yet he is making the almost impossible effort to finish the picture."

Joan Crawford also sympathized with Gable's problems, often checking with his secretary to ask how he was. Finally she sent him a note, inviting him to stop by her house for cocktails. Crawford's account of his visit was that Gable "talked for hours, talked and talked and talked. He'd listened to me once; now I listened to him, knitted, listened and filled the ice bucket. The next day I received twelve dozen red roses with the longest stems I'd ever seen."

When Gable began stopping at Crawford's house almost daily over the next few months, rumors started that their one-time affair had resumed. But Crawford's description of those meetings offers a different picture. "He wasn't the gay, romantic Clark I'd first known, he wasn't the easygoing Clark, he was a moody man who needed friendship."

"You're living in the past," Crawford said she told Gable. "You have a guilt complex because you didn't go with Carole on that trip. You couldn't go, you were working! You've had your grief, Clark, now pull yourself out of it."

But it was not that easy for Gable. There were too many painful reminders of Lombard. When "To Be or Not to Be" was released, the press was filled with new tributes to Lombard, hailing her excellent performance and bemoaning anew her premature death. She was rapidly becoming a national heroine. In a *Liberty* Magazine article entitled "Gallant Lady," Adela Rogers St. Johns said that Lombard "can symbolize to a nation which just happened to know and love her, better than some of the other heroes who have already fallen, the first great personal chance to catch the stride of the martial music to which all must march now." Lombard was honored in another way by a Navy air squadron called "The Lombardiers," whose insignia was Lombard's profile superimposed on an outline of her native state of Indiana.

A souvenir magazine, "Carole Lombard's Life Story," appeared suddenly and anonymously on newsstands, without any hint of its authorship or publisher. The magazine opened with an account of Gable seeing Lombard off on her bond tour at the train station and giving her "a kiss of which the Hays Office would not have approved." This scene, which of course never happened, was a source of anguish to Gable, who wished now that it had.

Gable's continuing depression was a matter of great concern to his friends. It was almost as if his own life had ended when Lombard was killed. Despite his doctor's warnings, he was drinking heavily and spending his nights running Lombard's old movies on a projector she'd once given him for Christmas or thumbing through the voluminous scrapbooks she'd kept of their life together.

At Gable's rare public appearances, Lombard's ghost usually accompanied him. In June 1942, he attended the funeral of John Barrymore, who had done so much to help Lombard's career when they worked together in "Twentieth Century." Later in the year, another of his wife's mentors, Buck Jones, died as tragically as Lombard had, while trying to rescue patrons in a Boston nightclub fire.

Gable, in no mood to continue his movie career, told his friends that he couldn't possibly face a camera again, that the reality of recent events made acting impossible. Since it had been Lombard's fondest wish that he should go into the service, he started giving it serious consideration.

But with so many of MGM's younger stars being drafted, its need to hold on to Gable was more urgent than ever. In an attempt to dissuade him from going into the service, the studio offered to star him in a film biography of flying ace Eddie Rickenbacker, which MGM claimed would boost public morale.

But Gable wanted no part of it. After he finished "Somewhere

I'll Find You," he started looking into the various military assignments that were open to him. "I don't want to sell bonds, I don't want to make speeches and I don't want to entertain," Gable said. "I just want to be sent where the going is tough."

A chance meeting with an Army Air Force officer in a restaurant decided Gable on his future course. In relating how difficult it was to recruit air gunners, Colonel Luke Smith suggested that Gable set an example by becoming one himself. "Everyone wants to be a pilot," the colonel told Gable, "but you'd be doing a real service as a gunner. It would help to glorify the plane crews and the grease monkeys." Since it sounded to Gable like something that Carole Lombard once had in mind for him, he followed through on the colonel's suggestion.

The thought of "The King of Hollywood" going into the service as an enlisted man at first appalled MGM, until it saw the publicity value of its $7,500-a-week star's giving it all up for the Air Force's $66 a month. Actually, though, Gable never had to make quite that sacrifice. Unpublicized, MGM paid him $150,000 a year while he was in the service to strengthen its hold on him when his military leave was over.

Gable's induction was delayed when he couldn't pass the physical examination. Despite the repairs that had been done at Johns Hopkins, the Army medics insisted on more dental work before he could be accepted, and it wasn't until August 1942 that he became Private Clark Gable. Inducted at the same time as Gable was Andy McIntyre, a studio cameraman whom MGM had secretly persuaded the Army to send along with Gable to ease his adjustment to military life.

Since Gable was receiving $150,000 a year from MGM, he could afford to retain his household staff to care for the ranch during his absence. He couldn't face up to selling it because of Lombard. "It would seem like letting her go forever," Gable said.

fifteen

The Last Wish of Carole Lombard

When Clark Gable went into service he took a special memento of Carole Lombard with him. Her ruby-and-diamond clips, which had been found in the wreckage of her plane, were mounted in a tiny gold box that he wore around his neck. When Gable was issued his dogtag—serial number o-565390—he had it fixed up with a metal cover, so that he could carry a picture of his wife inside.

Gable's decision to enlist was opposed by some of his friends. Victor Fleming, who'd directed him in "Gone With the Wind," and had hoped to persuade him to do the Rickenbacker biography, said, "How can that guy make better use of himself: by trying to do something any healthy twenty-year-old kid can do better or by telling the story of our greatest fighting flyer?" But while reproaching Gable, Fleming made a hero of him in the same breath. "We've had giants like Marconi, Steinmetz, Edison and Ford in this century," Fleming said, "but when this present era becomes as remote as the Stone Age is now, they'll still be talking about Gable. He will be a bigger American legend than Paul Bunyan and all the rest of them combined. He's the representative man of our time. No one will ever forget him."

Whether Gable's enlistment was an escape from unhappy

memories or the fulfillment of Lombard's last wish, he immediately regretted the decision, because it was the hardest task he had ever undertaken in his life. At forty-one, he was ill-equipped to compete with men half his age. And as "The King of Hollywood," he was to suffer many indignities and hardships when reduced to the rank of a private.

Gable was sent to the Officers' Candidate School near Miami, Florida, and at first there was a circus atmosphere about his enlistment. En route, word of his travels spread from city to city. In New Orleans, hundreds of screaming women encircled him at the railroad terminal, forcing him to miss his train connection. After he arrived in Florida, he was furious when the Army made a public spectacle out of his first haircut. Dozens of photographers and newsreel cameramen stood by while his head was shaved and the world's most famous moustache was removed.

After that, Gable was left alone. Not even the Army was about to publicize "The King" scrubbing floors or cleaning latrines. But he did mind the interrogations the officers put him through in front of his fellows. He was asked the most embarrassing and insulting questions, which he tried to answer calmly, without showing how much they ruffled him. Gable's most trying moments, though, happened when he was on guard duty. The women who worked or lived on the base marched along with him on the other side of the fence, giggling and tossing him scraps of paper with their telephone numbers on them. The situation proved so embarrassing to him that the Army was finally forced to post an official notice that Gable "will appreciate it if the public will not interfere with his training. He wishes to be treated like every other member of the Service."

But because he was Clark Gable, he received more than his share of rough treatment. In his squadron was a skinny little officer who constantly picked on Gable. During inspection he would wet his thumb and smear it across the brass buckle that Gable had polished to a high sheen, and Gable could do nothing but stand there at attention while the officer gave him a demerit.

Gable also had to overcome the diffidence of his fellow rookies, who didn't know how to react to this celebrated and much older man. Gable tried to prove to them that he wasn't any better than they were. In the washroom one morning, he took out his upper plate of false teeth and waved it at the other men. "Look at the King," he said laughingly, "the King of Hollywood. Sure looks like the Jack now, doesn't he?"

As the men got to know Gable better, they spoke glowingly of him. Said one, "Gable did not like people to paw him or yes him. But he would do anything for you. Once I was sick and he saw that I was fed. When we went out together, he did not grab the check. But you knew this was out of consideration for your pride. If we'd go out, it was fifty-fifty. We borrowed from each other and always paid back. The Army didn't give him a damned thing. I never saw him mad. But I saw him assert himself."

The physical regimen was very hard on the middle-aged Gable, who was awakened at 4:15 every morning and required to march a mile or two before breakfast. His perseverance through the endless drilling and exercise was partly because of his intense memories of Lombard, who would never have allowed such a situation to defeat her.

Gable was almost undone, however, by the academic side of his training. Never a good student, and a high school dropout in the tenth grade, he found it extremely difficult, at age forty-one, to adapt to a classroom routine. The curriculum included military law, transportation, supply, correspondence, kitchen, speech and education. If he failed, Gable was subject not only to being transferred to the infantry, but also to national humiliation if the truth was ever revealed.

Gable finally tackled the problem by treating his lessons as if they were movie scripts, memorizing them page by page. After "lights out" call at night, he would tuck a book under his robe and go out into the lavatory. Locking himself in a booth, he would sit on the toilet for hours, cramming for his next exam.

But in between classes, there were occasional diversions. Gable couldn't resist the advances of some of the women on the base. One, an officer's sister, who wore thick glasses and had the build of a lady wrestler, seemed an unlikely companion for Clark Gable. When a friend asked him how he could bother with such an unattractive woman, Gable said, "She makes no trouble. Sometimes the homely ones are the best kind, easy to please and very grateful afterwards."

Gable finished Officers' Candidate School 700th in a class of 2,600. In October 1942, after receiving his commission as an Air Force first lieutenant, he was sent to gunnery school, where his shooting skill was to make the regimen much easier for him. Flying, though, was a problem. Since Lombard's death, Gable had become plane-shy. It took many hours of flight time before he was able to overcome his nervousness.

Now that he was an officer, Gable was able to have his uniforms custom made. MGM supplied his wardrobe for the rest of his service, which made him just about the best-dressed man in the military. He also let his moustache grow back.

Just before Christmas 1942, Gable was granted his first leave, which he decided to spend at the ranch. He had a few anxious moments over Texas, when his plane developed engine trouble and he thought he was going to die in the same way as Lombard, but an emergency landing was made safely.

While he was home, Gable saw only a few intimate friends and passed the time roaming the ranch. Although tanned and robust-looking from his training period, he was in a melancholy mood. Every conversation eventually got around to Carole Lombard and a retelling of little episodes in their life together. Before he returned to his base, Gable told his secretary, "You know, I have everything in the world anyone could want but one thing. All I really need and want is Ma."

Upon graduation from gunnery school in January 1943, Gable received his silver wings. The following month he was assigned by General "Hap" Arnold to command a photographic unit to produce a documentary film on aerial gunnery, to be used for recruiting and training purposes.

Together with a crew of cameramen and technicians, Gable was flown to England, where he was based with the 351st Bomber Group and promoted to the rank of captain. Though the promotion was widely publicized, it was only a matter of routine. U.S. losses were so heavy at that time that men were being moved swiftly up the ranks.

As usual, Gable's arrival in a new setting caused him many harassments. Women from neighboring farms and villages collected at the gates to the base, following him whenever he went out. His superior officers vied with each other to have him as their dinner guest to show him off to their friends. Gable was particularly annoyed by the Air Force's efforts to glamorize him, which he knew would have infuriated Carole Lombard. With so many younger men being killed and maimed before his eyes, he felt silly and inadequate over his film-making assignment.

Although induction publicity had created the impression that Gable was going to be a regular aerial gunner, he never actually served in that capacity. That did not mean, however, that he never saw combat. Acting as a cameraman for the film unit he had brought over with him, he flew many dangerous missions over Europe. In August 1943, he took part in a huge raid into Germany aboard a Flying Fortress called "Ain't It Gruesome?" Gable spent the entire seven-hour flight taking pictures, wedged in behind the top turret gunner. Gable's plane sustained five Nazi attacks, returning to base with fifteen flack holes in the fuselage. During the flight, a 20 mm. shell tore through the floor near Gable, ripped off his boot heel and went out through the roof a foot from his head.

In another mission over Nantes, France, Gable operated the nose gun while over the target. Nazi fighters came so close that at one moment Gable said, "I could see the German pilot's features. That guy won't be around very long if he keeps on doing that. I don't know how we missed him, though. I didn't hit a damn thing myself."

In October 1943, Gable received the Distinguished Flying Cross and the Air Medal, the latter for "exceptionally meritorious achievement while participating in five separate bomber combat missions."

The prominent attention accorded Gable's military service did not go unnoticed by the Nazis, who placed him on their list of most wanted "war criminals." Although MGM had never, for obvious reasons, publicized the fact, Adolf Hitler had once made it known that Gable was his favorite American film actor.

A great movie fan, Hitler had a large collection of American films, many pirated from ocean liners before the war. Part of the Führer's fondness for "The King" was Gable's German ancestry. Gable's original family name, in fact, was Goebel. During Hitler's rise in the early Thirties, the MGM publicity department had changed references to Gable's heritage from German to Dutch, since there was a chance he might even be distantly related to the Nazi propaganda minister, Joseph Goebbels.

One of Gable's greatest fears was that the Nazis would capture him. He told a friend that if his plane was ever shot down, he would not bail out. "If I ever fall into Hitler's hands, the sonovabitch will put me in a cage like a big gorilla," Gable said. "He'd exhibit me all over Germany."

Air Minister Hermann Goering posted the equivalent of a $5,000 reward for the Nazi flyer who would bring Gable down. If Gable was captured alive, the flyer was also to receive a promotion and a furlough with all expenses paid.

Gable was part of a group called "Hatcher's Chickens," commanded by Colonel William Hatcher. The Nazis were apparently well informed of Gable's movements. One night, while Gable was at mess, Lord Haw Haw, the traitorous Englishman who broadcasted propaganda for the Nazis in the same way that Tokyo Rose did for the Japanese, said on the radio, "Welcome to England, Hatcher's Chickens, among whom is the famous American cinema star, Clark Gable. We'll be seeing you soon in Germany, Clark. You will be welcome there, too."

But Gable returned to the United States before the Nazis could claim him. By the end of 1943, he had accumulated about 50,000 feet of color film for the gunnery documentary. The footage included not only aerial combat but also scenes of daily life on the base and interviews with members of the raiding crews.

Gable had worked very hard on the project. "He had his whole heart and soul in it and said he was going to get the pictures he wanted even if Jerry dropped a bomb down the back of his neck," according to one of the men in his group. "Clark really loved the boys on the base. When one of them he'd been using in the film was killed on a mission, he gave up a leave to stay behind to write the man's widow a letter of condolence."

Despite his captain's rank, Gable maintained no special living quarters, insisting on sharing the other men's wooden barracks. They all called Gable "Pappy," which had been one of Carole Lombard's pet names for him.

In November 1943, the Air Force flew Gable to Washington to file a report with the War Department on the status of his film project. With dozens of photographers and reporters attending a press conference held in his honor, he was treated like a conquering hero. He was infuriated and mortified, claiming that he didn't deserve the tribute, that "other men had done so much more."

Gable returned to California for the editing of his film. After another hero's welcome at the railroad station, he rushed home to the ranch. It was a year since his last visit and nearly two years since Carole Lombard's death. Her rooms, still kept exactly as she left them, were the first place Gable went. His happiness over his homecoming turned to sadness as he realized anew that nothing had changed, that Lombard was never coming back.

Friends noticed that Gable was thinner and more serious now, that his hair was turning gray at the temples. Conversations often turned to his war experiences. "I saw so much in the way of death and destruction," Gable once said, "that I realized that I hadn't been singled out for grief—that others were suffering and losing their loved ones just as I lost Ma."

While awaiting the shipment of his film from Europe, Gable puttered around the ranch. There was talk of his being sent to the Pacific theater once his film was completed. When he paid a visit to MGM, he found that he was still "King," and as he walked into the commissary in uniform, the diners gave him a standing ovation. An observer said that "Richard the Lionhearted didn't get a better reception when he came back from the Crusades."

Although Gable was officially posted to the headquarters of the photographic division of the Air Corps at the Hal Roach

Studios, he did most of the work on his film at MGM. Five training and educational shorts were made from the footage. But by the time they were finished, they were considered obsolete, and they never received wide distribution.

Despite his still being in uniform, MGM renewed its contract with Gable for another seven years at $7,500 a week. He was also granted two concessions that Carole Lombard had been after him about for years—four months' vacation between pictures and the right to stop work at five o'clock in the afternoon. Involving a commitment by MGM of over $2,000,000, the deal evidenced the studio's faith in Gable's continuing popularity, despite his advancing years and his nearly two-year absence from the screen.

In January 1944, the U.S. Treasury Department, which had sponsored Carole Lombard's bond tour, announced that it was naming a new Liberty ship after her. Gable was invited to be the guest of honor at the 10,500-ton vessel's launching, which was to commemorate the second anniversary of Lombard's death and open a new bond drive.

The ceremony was held at the Terminal Island docks of the California Shipbuilding Corporation. More than fifteen thousand shipyard workers and their families attended the launching, which was staged with the help of MGM, with none other than Louis B. Mayer himself as the master of ceremonies and Fieldsie Lang as the matron of honor. Actress Irene Dunne, who had no close ties to Carole Lombard but just happened to be making a picture at MGM at that time, was selected to christen the ship.

Mayer eulogized Carole Lombard, citing her record of over $2,000,000 in bond sales as still unbroken. Gable, dressed in his newest custom-made uniform, listened with his head bowed, clenching his fists until they turned white. When it came to his own brief speech, he was too overcome by emotion to mention Lombard's name, speaking instead about the Liberty ships and the importance of shipbuilding to the war effort. The Liberty ship *Carole Lombard* was the 318th of its kind to be built at the California yards.

As Irene Dunne cracked a bottle of champagne against the prow and the ship began sliding from its berth, Gable snapped to attention and saluted, tears streaming down his cheeks. It was the first and only time that he ever made a public display of his grief over Carole Lombard's death.

Had it been a movie, that might have been the end of the Gable-Lombard love story. To the swelling of patriotic music, the camera would have pulled back for one final shot of the solitary Gable watching the U.S.S. *Carole Lombard* steam out to sea. But the real ending would not come until this haunted man's own death, sixteen years later.

sixteen

Looking for Another Lombard

Clark Gable spent the rest of his life with Carole Lombard's ghost. After his discharge from the Air Force in June 1944, he went into a long period of decline, drinking heavily and unable to face a future without Lombard. Finally, when he realized that there was no way of bringing her back, that he was destroying himself by mourning over her, he went looking for another Carole Lombard.

Gable's depression during the early postwar years was intensified by career problems. Although he continued unchallenged as "The King of Hollywood" and his name still meant automatic box-office success, the films that he made were, for the most part, undistinguished. He was never again to reach the heights of "Gone With the Wind," "It Happened One Night," "Mutiny on the Bounty" or many of the other memorable pictures he'd made in the Thirties.

Gable's life without Lombard reached its nadir in two incidents in the mid-Forties. Gable was often downing a fifth or a quart of Scotch before dinner. One friend said that he must have had "twenty pounds of blotting paper in his stomach" to absorb such enormous quantities of alcohol. Early one morning, after a long

night of boozing, Gable lost control of his car and crashed into a
tree on Sunset Boulevard. Although his injuries were not serious, he
was covered with blood. Two MGM publicists managed to get to
the crash scene before the police did, thus keeping the incident out
of the newspapers. The studio was so concerned over Gable's
drunken recklessness that when he was taken to the hospital, he was
kept there against his will until he had thoroughly dried out. All his
clothes were taken from him to guard against his trying to check
out ahead of time.

Gable also was involved in a minor scandal that hurt his pride
as a sportsman and distressed him greatly. He was charged with
breaking the California game laws by killing twenty-five ducks
when the limit was four. Although it was later shown that Gable
was framed and that the crime was really perpetrated by other
members of his gun club, the incident so outraged his sense of fair
play that he resigned from the gun club and for a long time lost all
interest in hunting, the sport he had enjoyed so much with Carole
Lombard.

Gradually, Gable began to shake off his depression. He was
seen more frequently at nightclubs and parties. Still the most
idolized movie star in the world, he once again found himself in the
forefront of Hollywood's eligible bachelors. Throughout the late
Forties, he was linked with many women, more often than not
blondes like Carole Lombard. But even when they weren't, there
was always something Lombardish about their appearance or personality that seemed to attract Gable to them. Quite a few of
Gable's girls were actresses or models—Virginia Grey, Marilyn
Maxwell, Paulette Goddard, Kay Williams, Audrey Totter, Anita
("The Face") Colby. Some were socialites like Dolly O'Brien and
Millicent Rogers. Many more were anonymous waitresses, bar-
maids and prostitutes that he met during his drunken carousing.

In December 1949, a month before the eighth anniversary of
Carole Lombard's death, Gable thought he'd found a surrogate for
his late wife and married her. She was a blue-eyed blonde like Lombard and, at forty-one, the same age her predecessor would have

been. Well known in international café society, she also had some
of Lombard's wit, high spirits and fashion flair. Her name was
Lady Sylvia Ashley.

The fourth Mrs. Gable had had quite a past. Born a poor
London cockney, she'd been an underwear model and chorus girl
before snaring her wealthy first husband, Lord Anthony Ashley,
heir of the Earl of Shaftesbury. While still wed to Lord Ashley, she
had an affair with silent-movie "King" Douglas Fairbanks, which
led to the break-up of his marriage to Mary Pickford. Ironically, it
was the failure of this "perfect" match that later led Hollywood
to attach such significance to the successful Gable-Lombard marriage. As soon as they were both divorced, Lady Ashley became
Mrs. Douglas Fairbanks, and remained so until his death in 1939.
After inheriting a million dollars from Fairbanks, she married another titled Britisher, Baron Stanley of Alderly. Upon their divorce
in 1948, she reverted to using the name of her first husband, Lord
Ashley.

Lady Ashley was the epitome of the gay divorcee when she
met Gable at a cocktail party two months before they were married.
Immediately taken by her striking physical resemblance to Carole
Lombard, Gable noticed other similarities when they started keeping company. He liked her sense of humor and her ability to laugh
at life and its little upsets in the same way that Lombard did.

The Gable-Ashley marriage—the fourth for both of them—
was a disaster almost from the start, lasting barely sixteen months.
Gable soon discovered he'd made a mistake, that he had little in
common with his new wife and that her regal, uppity ways made
her Lombard's exact opposite.

The trouble started right after the honeymoon, when Gable
brought Lady Ashley to live in the house that was virtually un-
changed from the way Carole Lombard left it. Lady Ashley immediately started making renovations that displeased Gable. She
turned his gun room into a frilly, chintz-curtained den that one
friend said resembled "the reception hall of a French whorehouse."
She replaced many of Carole Lombard's Early American pieces with

English antiques of her own. She completely remodeled his former wife's bedroom suite and toned down the leathery, masculine atmosphere that Lombard had striven so hard to achieve throughout the house. The end result, more London Mayfair than California Rancho, did not suit Gable's relaxed, informal life style.

Gable and his lady also came into conflict when she tried to dismiss some of the servants that had originally been hired by Carole Lombard. Gable was particularly fond of Martin, his black valet, whom Lady Ashley wanted to replace with an English butler. Gable was able to save Martin's job only by permitting his new wife to hire a personal maid. He was angered by the added expense, couldn't understand why Lady Ashley wasn't able to dress herself or run her own bath, as Carole Lombard did.

Gable, who led such a quiet, sheltered life with Carole Lombard, also objected to the very active social calendar that Lady Ashley devised for them. He hated the constant parties with members of the international smart set and the frequent trips to the opera, during which he usually fell asleep. He was annoyed by the incessant visits of Lady Ashley's numerous relatives, who further intruded on his privacy.

But what soured Gable most on the marriage was his realization that Lady Ashley could never take Carole Lombard's place. This shortcoming was not, of course, Ashley's fault, but Gable didn't understand that. In her own way, Ashley tried to enter into Gable's kind of life. She went hunting and fishing with him, but loathed it. When she accompanied Gable to the remote Colorado location of "Across the Wide Missouri," her idea of roughing it was to take twenty-seven pieces of luggage with her. She made life miserable for the film's crew by demanding that they transform a perfectly comfortable little guest house into a palatial villa, with fresh turf, trees and flowers, all the latest electrical appliances, and frilly curtains on the windows. Gable cringed, remembering some of the broken-down shacks that Carole Lombard had been content to stay in during their hunting trips. Gable was also constantly ribbed by the film crew over Ashley's habit of bringing her pet

Chihuahua to the communal dining table. The dog wore a tiny diamond collar, a gift from Gable before he woke up to the mistake he'd made in marrying Lady Ashley.

The final break came after a surprise dinner party that Lady Ashley held for Gable on his fiftieth birthday. The menu was to include Gable's favorite dish, chicken and dumplings. A newly hired cook prepared the chicken a day ahead and it spoiled when she failed to refrigerate it properly. Gable gasped when he took his first bite of the rancid food, rose angrily from the table, glared at Lady Ashley and locked himself in his room for the balance of the evening.

Divorce proceedings were started in May 1951. Lady Ashley said that Gable had told her, "I don't want to be married to you any longer. Or to anyone else." She claimed that during their brief marriage Gable made her suffer many indignities, not the least of which was forcing her to live in the shadow of Carole Lombard.

Fearing that Lady Ashley would try to fleece him of everything he had, Gable immediately established residence in Nevada and attempted to transfer all his assets out of California. He wanted to avoid, if he could, the traumatic experience of his earlier divorce settlement with Ria Gable. Legal skirmishing dragged on for almost a year before an agreement was reached. Although no figure was ever announced, it was believed that Lady Ashley came out of the marriage about a quarter of a million dollars richer.

Gable's greatest fear had been that Lady Ashley would take the ranch, which meant so much to him because of its ties with Carole Lombard. As soon as that threat was removed, Gable undid most of Lady Ashley's renovations. His guns went back on the walls in the den, the living room was restored to Lombard's original color scheme, her bedroom suite was changed back to the way it had been before Lady Ashley took it over.

After the divorce, Gable again became very depressed, this time over the failure of the marriage and the subsequent drain on his bank account. In an attempt to recoup some of his losses, he worked out a deal with MGM to make his next three pictures outside the United States. By remaining out of the country for eighteen months, his salary during that period would be exempt from income taxes.

After making "Never Let Me Go" in England, Gable proceeded to East Africa for "Mogambo," a remake of "Red Dust," in which he'd starred opposite Jean Harlow in 1934. Harlow's part was being played by Ava Gardner, who was accompanied to the location by her husband, Frank Sinatra. The singer's career was not going well at the time. Very jealous of Gardner, he'd come along to make sure that she did not become romantically involved with Gable.

Sinatra's suspicions proved groundless, for Gable's interest was focused exclusively on Grace Kelly, the twenty-three-year-old blonde who had the second female lead in "Mogambo." She was not only beautiful, but a fine sportswoman and a crack shot, and she reminded Gable a great deal of Carole Lombard. Her frequent hunting expeditions with Gable developed into a close relationship. Grace Kelly called Gable "Ba," the Swahili word for "Father," which wasn't far off from Lombard's "Pa."

The Gable-Kelly association continued on and off for some time after "Mogambo" was completed. Gable seriously considered marrying Grace Kelly, but eventually realized that the twenty-eight-year age difference between them was too great. Kelly, however, would probably not have accepted Gable's proposal. While she found much to admire in "The King," she reportedly could never get accustomed to his false teeth. Three years later, she married into real royalty and retired from the screen.

Returning to Hollywood at the end of 1953, Gable suffered his greatest upset since the death of Carole Lombard. After an association of twenty-three years, MGM advised Gable that it would not renew his contract when it expired early in 1954. Although Gable's fifty MGM films had done more to enrich the studio than any other star's, the company could no longer afford him. Since the end of World War II and the advent of television, movie attendance had declined sharply, while production costs had increased alarmingly. All of the major studios—and MGM in particular because it was the largest—were forced to retrench. The trend now was toward retaining stars on a picture-by-picture basis. Since long-term contractees like Gable had to be paid even while not working, the new hiring practice saved the studios a great deal of money.

Gable was bitter over his break with MGM, although he eventually realized it was probably for the best. The studio operation had changed drastically in the postwar years and Gable felt like a stranger amidst all the new faces. He was the last important holdover from the Thirties. Even Louis B. Mayer had been bounced. Gable had no use for Dore Schary, Mayer's replacement, or for any of the younger guard at MGM.

On his last day at MGM, Gable grumbled to a friend, "I bet those big shots in the front office won't even give me a goodbye lunch, after all the millions of bucks they've made with me." He lost the bet. A luncheon was held, but when Gable got up to speak, all he would say was "I wish to pay tribute to my friends and associates who are no longer alive."

Not long after Gable left MGM, "Mogambo" proved such a box-office hit that the studio wanted to hire him back. Gable refused, telling his agent, "See how high you can get those sons-of-bitches to go. When you get their very best offer, tell them to take the money, their studio, their cameras and lighting equipment and shove it all up their ass."

That statement sounded more like Carole Lombard than Clark Gable. When she was having such success as a free-lance star, Lombard had often advised Gable to break away from MGM and follow her example. Then too insecure to risk it, he was sorry that he hadn't taken her advice. From then on, he did, receiving a very substantial guarantee plus a percentage of the profits on the nine pictures he was to make as a free-lance star in the next few years.

Although Gable had said after the Lady Ashley fiasco that he would never marry again, he did, in July 1955, at age fifty-four. This time the resemblance to Carole Lombard was much more than superficial. The fifth Mrs. Gable was thirty-nine-year-old Kay Williams, a former Powers model and actress, one of the blue-eyed blondes he'd been dating on and off for years.

Kay Williams had been in love with Gable ever since she'd first met him at MGM in 1942, not long after Lombard's death. But just as there'd been a long hiatus between Gable and Lombard's first meeting and their romance, it had taken him years to wake up to Kay Williams' potentialities. When she finally married Gable, Kay Williams had been divorced three times, and had two children by her third husband, millionaire sugar heir Adolph Spreckels, Jr.

Unlike Lady Ashley, Kay Williams did not try to fight Carole Lombard's ghost. Instead, she turned herself into another Carole Lombard: she swore like her, dressed like her, subordinated herself to Gable exactly as Lombard had done. A close friend, who'd known both Lombard and Williams, said, "Sometimes I could close my eyes and listen to Clark and Kay call each other Ma and Pa and exchange quips and insults, and I thought I was listening to a road version of the Gable-Lombard marriage." Even the Gable-Williams wedding resembled the earlier Gable-Lombard one. Again it was an elopement, with Gable sending a friend out in advance to find a remote spot where the lovers could be married without fanfare and publicity.

Gable took Kay Williams back to live at the ranch, although they talked of selling it, fearful of the effect Carole Lombard's ghost might have on their marriage. But his new wife knew it would break Gable's heart to leave the place. "You love the ranch, Pa," she told him. "I love the ranch. It's an ideal place to bring up children. Let's not think of moving."

Gable's years with Kay Williams—he called her Kathleen—were probably the happiest of his life. She not only gave him back the companionship and contentment he'd known with Carole Lombard, but also presented him with the one thing Lombard hadn't—a family. He became devoted to her two young children, Bunker and Joan, treating them as if they were his own.

Late in 1955, Gable learned that he was to have a child of his own. Kay Gable miscarried, however, and remained in poor health for a long time afterward, her condition complicated by heart trouble. There were many moments when Gable thought he was going to lose her. But Kay Gable was luckier than Carole Lombard. She survived the worst crisis of her life, seemingly the stronger for it.

In 1957, Gable celebrated his twenty-fifth anniversary as a star. Now fifty-six, he had made sixty pictures since 1930, when he started as a featured player. While still unchallenged as "The King," he was beginning to appear ludicrous playing the same kind of dashing, romantic roles opposite leading ladies a generation or two younger than he was. Though he often talked of retirement, money still meant too much to him. With his percentage deals, he was making more than he'd ever earned at MGM.

The pattern of Gable's life continued pretty much as it had with Carole Lombard—several months out for a film and then long periods of relaxation and hunting trips with his wife. The painful memories of Lombard's death gradually subsided, though there were moments that brought them back. When Elizabeth Taylor's husband, showman Mike Todd, was killed in an air crash in 1958, Gable was one of the first to offer help. He was on the phone with Elizabeth Taylor for an hour, consoling her and giving her the benefit of his own experience in the Carole Lombard tragedy.

In 1960 came the most tempting offer of Gable's career—$750,-000 plus a percentage to appear in "The Misfits," an original screenplay by Arthur Miller to be directed by John Huston. Gable saw the project as a partial means of making up for the fortune he felt he'd been deprived of by not having an interest in "Gone With the Wind." The deal on "The Misfits" was so advantageous—including a bonus of $48,000 for each week the picture might go into overtime shooting—that Gable never stopped to listen to friends who warned him that he would have nothing but trouble with his neurotic leading lady, Marilyn Monroe.

It was only fitting that Marilyn Monroe—the last woman to play a decisive role in Clark Gable's life—should be a blue-eyed blonde like all the others he'd been involved with since Carole Lombard. Monroe, at thirty-four, was just a few months older than Lombard was when she died. Her resemblance to Lombard, especially when she dressed in jeans and wore her hair in pigtails, was striking.

Monroe, then near the breaking point of her marriage to Arthur Miller, was under great emotional stress. She probably should have been undergoing psychiatric treatment in a sanitarium instead of making a new movie. Her tantrums, indecisions and generally unprofessional behavior during the filming of "The Misfits" were to cause many delays and ultimately wear Gable down. There seemed to be nothing malicious about her conduct, because Monroe was in awe of Gable. As an orphan child, she had carried his picture around with her, claiming that he was her father.

Gable was fifty-nine when he started "The Misfits." For some time, his age had been catching up with him. He was now puffy in the face and paunchy around the waist, his hands shook a great deal and he was having trouble learning lines. Whether the tremors were caused by his years of hard drinking or a sign of advancing Parkinson's disease, Gable was in no condition to endure the nervous tensions created by Marilyn Monroe's erratic moods.

Day after day, as she popped tranquilizers in alarming numbers and found it increasingly difficult to arrive on the set, Marilyn Monroe kept Clark Gable waiting. When she left him sitting interminably in the rarefied 110-degree heat of the Nevada desert location, Gable must have felt Carole Lombard's ghost closing in on him again. Looming majestically in the distance was the same mountain range where Lombard had died, eighteen years before. When a limousine pulled up in the hazy midday heat, the blonde stepping out of the car toward Gable could almost have been Carole Lombard. Instead, it was the tardy Marilyn Monroe, looking very much like Lombard in a skintight white silk dress.

During the filming of "The Misfits," Gable learned that his wife, Kay, was pregnant again. The child born was a boy—John Clark Gable. But the final irony of Gable's life was that he never saw his son. On November 16, 1960, Gable died of a heart attack, two weeks after "The Misfits" was completed. His son was not born until the following March.

Clark Gable had had no history of heart trouble. Though she didn't mention Marilyn Monroe by name, his widow said that "The Misfits" had "helped kill him." Kay Gable said, "It wasn't the physical exertion that did it. It was the horrible tension, that eternal waiting, waiting, waiting. He waited around forever, for everybody. He'd get so angry, waiting, that he'd just go ahead and do anything to keep occupied. That's why he did those awful horse scenes where they dragged him at twenty-five to thirty miles an hour behind a truck. He had a stand-in and a stunt man, but he did them himself. I told him 'You're crazy,' but he wouldn't listen."

When she learned of Mrs. Gable's accusations, Marilyn Monroe came close to killing herself. Eighteen months later she succeeded.

Due to his tenure in the Air Force, Clark Gable received a full military funeral. It was the same kind of ceremonial occasion that had once been offered Carole Lombard but rejected by Gable in keeping with the instructions in her will. The services for Gable were held in the same chapel as Lombard's, the Church of the Recessional at Forest Lawn. Some of Gable's peers were pallbearers—Spencer Tracy, Robert Taylor, James Stewart—mourning "The King" of them all. There would never be another one.

Taps was sounded as Clark Gable's coffin was lowered into the ground. He was buried next to Carole Lombard.

Acknowledgments

I am especially grateful to the many friends and colleagues of Clark Gable and Carole Lombard who contributed information and a frame of reference for this book. Listed alphabetically, they include: Eadie Adams, George L. Bagnall, Robert Baral, Jack Benny, Phil and Leila Berg, Pandro S. Berman, Clarence Bull, Stanley L. Campbell, Teet Carle, Claudette Colbert, William (Buster) Collier, Joan Crawford, Jean Dixon, John Engstead, Jean Garceau, Norris and Liz Goff, Edith Head, Andy Hervey, Arthur Hornblow, Jr., Cornwell Jackson, Madison Lacey, Myrna Loy, John Lee Mahin, Alice Marble, Peggy Mercer, Al Menasco, Lloyd Pantages, Frederic Peters, Walter Plunkett, Jill Winkler Rath, Adela Rogers St. Johns, Irene Selznick, Max Showalter, Donald Ogden Stewart, Howard Strickling, the late Joseph Szigeti, Dr. Franklyn Thorpe, King Vidor, Ruth Waterbury, William Wellman, Margaret Wyler and Jerome Zerbe.

Thanks also to Edward E. Slattery, Jr., of the National Transportation Safety Board, and to the staffs of the following research centers: the Library of the Performing Arts at Lincoln Center, New York; the Museum of Modern Art Film Library, New York; the Library of the Academy of Motion Picture Arts and Sciences, Los Angeles; the American Film Institute Library, Los Angeles; and the British Film Institute Library, London.

I am also indebted to the following for their help and encouragement in preparing this book: Barry Conley, Pamela Doyle, Norman Flicker, William C. Kenly, Steve Schwartz, Evelyn Seeff, Hy Smith and Bob Ullman. Most importantly, a special note of gratitude to Jerrold A. Weitzman.

Index